# PARALLEL LIVES

# PARALLEL LIVES

A Love Story from a Lost Continent

## IAIN PEARS

**W. W. NORTON & COMPANY**
*Independent Publishers Since 1923*

First published in Great Britain in 2025 by William Collins,
an imprint of HarperCollins.

Copyright © 2025 by Iain Pears

For information about permission to reproduce selections from this book, write to
Permissions, W. W. Norton & Company, Inc., 500 Fifth Avenue, New York, NY 10110

For information about special discounts for bulk purchases, please contact
W. W. Norton Special Sales at specialsales@wwnorton.com or 800-233-4830

Manufacturing by Lake Book Manufacturing

ISBN 978-1-324-07377-2

W. W. Norton & Company, Inc., 500 Fifth Avenue, New York, NY 10110
www.wwnorton.com

W. W. Norton & Company Ltd., 15 Carlisle Street, London W1D 3BS

1 2 3 4 5 6 7 8 9 0

*To LS*

*whole centuries separate the present from the days*
*I am about to depict*

François-René de Chateaubriand
*Memoirs from Beyond the Tomb*

# Contents

# List of Illustrations

All illustrations are from the Haskell Collection, unless otherwise stated.

# List of Illustrations

# Introduction

A few years ago, my old Russian friend Larissa Salmina Haskell showed me a sepia-tinted photograph that was lying on a pile of old newspapers. I asked who it was, this young boy in military uniform. 'Ah,' she replied, 'that's my cousin. He was eaten by a bear.'

She paused and looked at me carefully. 'It was a *white* bear,' she said, managing to convey the idea that to be eaten by any other sort of bear would have been indeed unfortunate. She often came out with unsettling remarks which generated far more questions than they managed to answer. On another occasion we were talking about the *Death of Stalin* and the portrayal of the utterly repellent and psychopathic Lavrentiy Beria, the head of the NKVD whose execution is the film's denouement.

Larissa nodded in agreement, then added for the sake of fairness: 'But we always quite *liked* Beria in my family.'

And how could anyone possibly like Beria?

'Well, you see, he murdered the man who tortured my uncle.'

Eventually, I persuaded her to tell me more, pointing out that it would be a pity if all of her memories were lost. She was already nearly 90 and, although it may have been tactless to hint that

1

Larissa's cousin: eaten by a bear

time was running short, she agreed that it really was a case of now or never. I went to visit regularly with a recorder and took down hours of reminiscences. She described how she was caught in the siege of Leningrad ('Cat's tail? Delicious'). She was evacuated over the ice, lived in the Urals surrounded by Spanish revolutionaries like La Pasionaria ('lovely woman'), went feral and fended for herself in the wreckage of Leningrad after the siege ('the happiest time of my life'), then rose to become one of the youngest Commissars in the Soviet Union and keeper of Venetian drawings at the Hermitage Museum. She took the Russian contribution to the Venice Biennale in 1962 and lost it on the journey. She briefly absconded with her supervisor's corpse, developed a useful sideline in forgery, and stole a Matisse ('I didn't steal it. I liberated it') from the Italian government.

And above all she met her husband, an art historian called Francis Haskell, and left her beloved Leningrad in 1965 with the help of the KGB to come and live in England.

This opened a story I had not expected, because laid out in her words was an extraordinary, and moving, love story played out against the backdrop of the Cold War. It brings back into sharp focus the strange world of the Soviet Union, and the even stranger world of a certain section of the English elite. It comprises two tales, one which begins in northern Russia, the other in Baghdad, and tries to describe how the daughter of a Soviet army officer from a noble family could meet the grandson of an Iraqi Jew with both instantly understanding each other so profoundly that they were prepared to risk heartbreak and, in her case, retribution, in order to be together. It is about how coming to England from the Soviet Union was a sacrifice, and how it was the English man, not the Russian woman, who was set free because of their meeting.

It is a tale of a Europe that is lost. Not the Europe of geographical and ideological divisions, but of a certain mentality, which was common to a very few on both sides of the Iron Curtain. When Francis went to Leningrad to meet her family, he recorded a dinner 'with Larissa's husband's mistress, who is one of Larissa's closest friends' (21 April 1963). It was all so familiar to him, as his friends in France and Italy and England were forever complaining that their mistresses were unfaithful or that their wives were being horrible to their new boyfriends. But more important were their common tastes and values. Art, ballet, theatre, music, books. Larissa's father took a complete set of Dickens with him to the

Battle of Kerch in Crimea; Francis knew Russian music and ballet inside and out. Both loved Paris; the reality for Francis, the idea of it for Larissa.

Whatever their differences in nationality, language and politics, both were members of a unified, pan-European culture which paid little heed to the divisions which so preoccupied most people of the age. They also operated by very different rules, and had very different values, to the societies in which they existed. It was a world of dancers, exiles and the occasional spy, of artists, aristocrats and academics. It consisted of people who felt safe only when they were away from home, were comfortable only in the company of foreigners.

---

I came to this project because Francis once taught me, and I was living nearby when he died in 2000. So I took to dropping in to check that Larissa was all right, and for the first time began to talk to her properly — she was always in the background while he was alive. Bit by bit, I stopped going out of duty, and began to visit out of pleasure. She was immensely entertaining, if occasionally alarming. This showed itself in her sometimes startling conversation — 'I must tell you about our first night of passion in Trieste' — but also in her activities. On one occasion she looted the house of a recently dead friend, taking away a large number of Russian paintings and drawings which she thought should have been left to the woman's niece in St Petersburg. These she sold through a London auction house, then laundered the money through the Swiss bank account of a Moscow art dealer. All of this she did without thinking twice. When I asked her if she realised quite how many laws she had just broken, she merely shrugged: 'I'm 82. What could they do to me?'

I began to see that she had an exceptional eye as well. She would flick through the catalogues of art shows, muttering 'good – fake – wrong', telling me as she turned the pages which dealers could be trusted, which were scoundrels. A lot were scoundrels. And every now and then she would go to the local auction house to buy some tatty picture. A lithograph, estimate £10, which she had spotted as an original watercolour by Léon Bakst, the Russian painter and stage designer. All of this with a rather girlish delight at her triumph, and no little pleasure at showing how much better she was at this sort of thing than I could ever dream of being.

I forgave her. She had a depth of knowledge which few now possess: no one has the time or leisure to study works of art with such intensity, over so many years. And that was the starting point of this project, which then expanded to chronicle not only a certain type of knowledge but also a particular way of living. It was not necessarily better, or richer than what we have now. But it was different, and it has gone forever.

I began to realise this loss fully when Larissa invited me to one of her New Year's Eve parties. She lived in a house covered in valuable works of art, but which had not been tidied for years. Books filled the shelves and were piled in unsteady stacks all over the floor, in the basement, the loft and on nearly every staircase. The lighting was a little dim, the room a little cold, and the chairs, arranged in a circle, were stiff-backed. I was some quarter of a century younger than everyone else; the others were old, old friends, contemporaries who were in tune with each other. I had not a clue.

They played pre-dinner games, but not of the sort that anyone plays now; not of the sort that anyone probably could play.

'*Marriage of Figaro*. Best performance.'

'Karl Böhm, Salzburg, 1958.'

'No. Böhm knew nothing of Mozart. Besides, the soprano was dreadful. Surely, Karajan in Vienna in 1967 was far superior.'

There was an argument defending Karl Böhm's honour and attacking Herbert von Karajan's egotism, then the next questioner came in.

'What meets where the Rhine loses his majestic force?'

There was no point in even mentioning that this was a quotation from an eighteenth-century poem by James Thomson. It was assumed (wrongly in my case) that everyone would know that. They had all read it at school, apart from Larissa. No one, however, could remember the answer. The questioner solved the problem – 'the Stork assembly' – with a distinct cry of triumph, and a muttering of 'oh, of course' from the others.

I was listening to the falling song of a dying world. Their experiences and their common heritage matched nothing I was familiar with. All had been formed before the age of consumerism dawned in Europe, and for their generation and background, money was merely one currency of exchange out of many. They had something much more valuable. Their wealth was in knowledge – they knew the Salzburg Festival existed when few had heard of it; knew people who would put them up, knew museum directors who would open the doors for them when a museum was closed to the public. But there was a price to this; it was an enclosed world, largely cut off from the rest of humanity, and about that they knew very little.

This book is also a study of how to survive the cruelty which is the dark side of this world; not only the gross variety of Stalin's Russia, with its arrests, murders, torture and pogroms, but also the more subtle and insidious type which was the English speciality. The coldness and indifference of family life; Eton in the 1940s, where Jews were hunted down and thrown into the river for sport; the superior malice of a Cambridge college

('I like second-rate minds: that's why I approve of Jesus'). The narrowness and misogyny of the social milieu, and its unique, highly developed ability to spot and exploit the least insecurity. When trying to convey the ritualised humiliations, discomfort and misery of life in the army, Francis noted that it reminded him of Eton.

For Francis was an insider who never completely belonged. Eventually he became Professor of the History of Art at Oxford and one of the most innovative and influential historians of his generation. He was awarded the *Légion d'honneur* by the French, medals by the British and Italians. He went from Eton to King's College Cambridge and was a member of the Apostles, that secretive debating society which produced the Cambridge spies. He counted E. M. Forster, Mary McCarthy, William Styron and Anthony Blunt among his friends. His was the world of Cambridge common rooms and London clubs. But he was a Jew who knew nothing of Judaism, an Englishman who knew little of England. And he lived in a world where friendship was always conditional, where he felt tormented by his Judaism and uncomfortable about his sexuality. His only contact with women was with well-brought-up English girls he found either vacuous or humourless, or the terrifyingly poised ballerinas presented to him by his ballet critic father. Larissa – equal in intellect, superior in skills, remarkably self-possessed and utterly charming – was unlike anyone he had ever encountered.

That they met at all – in a little restaurant in Venice in late August 1962 – was a small accident of history. That they fell deeply in love was entirely their own doing. Neither expected it, and neither particularly welcomed it. Certainly, Larissa never had the slightest desire to come permanently to the West. She was forever a daughter of Leningrad and remained doggedly loyal to her country, despite being all too aware of its flaws. And Francis

Francis and the French-Ukrainian dancer Nina Bibikova, Eton, 1946

had all but abandoned hope of ever being able to fall in love, or to find anyone who could love him.

My own role in writing this tale should be explained, as I occupy a midpoint between their world and the current one and see my task a little like an interpreter of one to the other. I went to university just before Mrs Thatcher took a sledgehammer to everything that Francis considered worthwhile. But I was born too late to feel comfortable with the values of his generation, and too early ever to adjust convincingly to the new world of competition and insecurity that replaced them. A sizeable portion of my life was lived as a European; I must have been one of the very first to take advantage of the Common Market by going to work for a period in a French factory in 1974. In some ways, some of the structure of the world I will be describing has returned recently; British citizens no longer have the right to wander Europe at will and for as long as they wish; the Cold War is back with a vengeance, though somewhat warmer. It is even possible that the less materialistic approach of some six decades ago may return as well under the pressure of environmental concerns and declining spending power. Mentally and emotionally, however, their world is gone. The international intelligentsia, of which they were both central members, has broken up, appreciation and knowledge of the things they esteemed has declined, the consensus over what is valuable and worthwhile in art, literature and music has collapsed.

Finding a suitable way of presenting this tale has been difficult, not least because the two principal characters do not even meet until near the very end. Once they married and settled down, their lives were happy, fulfilling, but similar to those of many an academic couple of the period. It was, certainly, the Golden Age of the University, offering a life which was far easier and much more pleasant than it is for academics today, but that is another story.

Equally, the evidence for each strand of the tale is very different. Larissa spent many hours sitting at her kitchen table, telling me stories while I listened, drank coffee, and prompted her with questions. Her account is inevitably from a distance, edited and shaped by memory and forgetfulness – it is difficult to believe that life during the siege of Leningrad was quite as jolly as the tone of her recollections sometimes suggested. Nor was she averse to omitting stories on occasion – for example, not mentioning her first marriage for more than two years out of concern for my natural delicacy.

In Francis's case there is little later testimony, but until Larissa arrived in England, his most reliable and steadfast friend was his diary, and there are some sixty volumes now deposited in the National Gallery in London, beginning while he was still at school and covering much of the next twenty years. Larissa not only allowed me to read these, she encouraged me to use them in whatever way I saw fit.

It is always difficult with such records to work out what the writer intended. The accounts may have begun as the private scribblings of a tormented and lonely adolescent – 'nobody knows me, except my diary' – but as they continued, this strand of self-examination was overlain with a more literary intent. Certainly, Francis was very keen to preserve them; when he was called up for his National Service at the end of 1946, he put the volumes in a deposit box at his bank – partly to ensure that his excessively nosy mother did not get her hands on them in his absence, but also because he thought them worth keeping. Towards the end of his life, he had the opportunity to destroy them had he wanted but did not do so. The many hours he spent writing them in fact helped shape his career – the value he placed on his own personal records made him far more sensitive to the importance of similar historical documents than were most art historians of his generation. That in turn made him more inclined to look after the ones he had produced himself. As he wrote in 1960: 'I suppose that reaching into other people's papers the whole time has helped to make me want to keep some of my own' (20 September).

While many of the entries simply record things said, done, seen or felt, occasionally they are more than that, and have the flavour of a literary set-piece. In other notebooks there are first and second drafts crafting a tale which strikes him as particularly memorable – he wrote two accounts, enormously and self-consciously funny, of the occasion he lost his virginity in a seedy Paris hotel to his landlady's daughter. Before he settled down to serious academic life, he had some ambitions to be a novelist or writer of short stories, but realised soon enough this was never going to be his calling. Many of his efforts in that direction were abandoned half-way through and are often too striving and literary; the characters wooden, the dialogue reminiscent of the 1930s intellectual novels he so frequently read and ultimately came to dislike. The journals are entirely different: rarely malicious, more often generous, they are fresh and keenly observed, with a splendid sense of the absurd, especially when he is describing himself: 'We discussed the formation of a new art movement the whole point of which was that it wasn't to be a movement … Can't honestly say I understood very much about it' (n.d. July 1949).

So, while Larissa's account is selective, shaped around the most notable events, and often lacking in particulars, his account is immediate and detailed. Her tale is tinged with the nostalgia of old age looking back on youth. That of Francis features the daily battle against the insecurities and confusions of youth as it was experienced. Taking account of these different perspectives is a tricky business.

Larissa had a quite remarkable and enviable ability to make people like her, a quality which is exceptionally difficult to pin down and explain. Nonetheless, it was very real: many years ago, the couple went to the Getty Foundation in California, and a party was thrown in their honour. Guests were invited to meet a great art historian, and on arrival one of these noticed a large group gathered around listening to a diminutive figure, who she assumed was the historian in question. It was Larissa, charming all around her, while Francis stood on the sidelines with his drink. This she managed in all circumstances, places and languages. Whether or not she was truly characteristic of Russians in general, I do not know. But it suggests that the powers-that-were in the

Soviet Union were wise in their decision to allow her to leave. Her presence in the West helped a little to bolster the idea of Russians as warm, cultivated, generous and just a little bit eccentric.

# 1

# Larissa: Background, Birth and Childhood, 1931–1941

*Birth – Home – Parties and Dancing – Moscow – Purges –
Promotion and Demotion – Torture – Hiding Under the
Table – Holidays – The Coming of the Germans*

The childhoods of Larissa and Francis were radically different, and for much of the time she experienced growing up in Stalin's Soviet Union as being much more agreeable than he found a privileged life in England. She was born on 27 February 1931, the only child of Nikolai Ivanovich Salmin and Vera Pavlovna Tarasova, in a hospital opposite the main Leningrad railway station, a proximity which she firmly believed was responsible for her love of travel in later life. Her father was 31 and came from the minor Russian nobility; the family had owned an estate near Dubrovka on the Neva River, and a grand house on Krestovsky Island in Leningrad. Her mother was eight years younger, and from a somewhat lower family; Vera's grandfather had been an estate manager for the immensely powerful Orlov family and her father a doctor who 'just left one wife for another'. He married Vera's mother because she was quite rich 'but then left her as well'. She died while Vera was young and the young girl was initially brought up on the Orlov estate. But this was razed to the ground during the Revolution and at the age of 9 Vera had to move to the city: 'She barely managed to finish school and then had to go to work, and her life was very difficult.' Until, that is, she met Nikolai Salmin in 1929 and he fell head over heels in love with her.

Nikolai by then was a colonel in the Red Army, but he had received the best education the Imperial Russian system could provide, joining the Kadetsky Korpus, a military academy founded by the Empress Anne in 1731 and abolished by the Bolsheviks in 1917. It was an elite institution – annual intake was around two hundred people and before the Revolution 90 per cent came from noble stock – and, like many such, it was noted for both the breadth and the brutality of the education it provided: 'It was worse than Eton was for Francis. It was so cruel.' But he survived and in 1917 threw in his lot with the Revolution – one of the few from the corps who did so – and made the transition from Czarism to Communism at the moment the new regime needed all the soldiers it could lay its hands on and wasn't too fussy where they came from. Besides, shortly before the Revolution broke out, he had transferred to study chemistry, and became a specialist in both artillery and chemical warfare, writing the textbook on the subject for the Red Army. This gave him a much-needed level of expertise and – though his progress was slowed by his family background – his career advanced, although with many reverses and near disasters. He had a fairly secure position, a good income, and was devotedly in love with Vera, all of which made him a fine catch. 'His character changed over the years because he became very gloomy, did not like people, and, in general, changed a lot. But at this time, just when he met my mother, he was a cheerful, sociable and relatively easy person.'

The Salmins were well born and well positioned, but even before the Revolution were not particularly rich, as Larissa's great-grandfather had gambled away much of the family fortune. Nikolai's elder brother, Yevgeny, joined the navy and ended up as a rear admiral, while the two brothers' father, Ivan Ivanovich, had been a general who played a prominent role in the disastrous 1905 war with Japan and was briefly Governor of Port Arthur. He

General Ivan Ivanovich Salmin

was not a pleasant person. 'He had a terrible character and so my father was quite unhappy ... his parents quarrelled all the time. His mother used to say that if you took all the bad qualities of her children and put them together, the result would still be better than her husband.' Unlike his children, Ivan refused to join the new regime. He did not have to, as in October 1917 he was on the Western Front, acting as a liaison officer with the French army. When the Bolsheviks took over, he decided to stay, mainly at the urging of his French mistress, whose charms greatly exceeded those of his wife back in Russia. After the war, he opened a brewery, which prospered for a few years, but in 1929 his wife persuaded him to come back to Leningrad as she had heard that the government was preparing to return confiscated property. The mistress agreed: 'You can recover your estates, sell them, then come back to Paris.' So he went, arriving shortly after Nikolai and Vera married. However, the rumour was untrue; no property was returned and when he saw what had been done to his houses – the estates razed, and the townhouse turned into multi-occupancy apartments – he was so overcome with rage that he had a heart attack and died just as his son was climbing the stairs to introduce him to his new daughter-in-law. Larissa had no idea what happened to the mistress, or the brewery.

She was an only child and surrounded by attention – as well as her mother, there was a nanny and her paternal grandmother, both of whom doted on her. Her grandmother was particularly important; she clung on in the family's Leningrad house, a beautiful Neoclassical wooden structure with painted columns which lasted until it was chopped up for firewood during the siege in 1942. The house was subdivided after 1917 and she was confined to a single room while newcomers were assigned the others, but the change made little difference to her approach to life: she simply treated all the new arrivals as either guests or servants depending on how much she liked them, continued to regard the whole building as her property, and was severe in her punishment of any who transgressed her rules.

For a while Larissa's parents lived there as well, but they moved out as Vera wanted to be near her friends in the centre of Leningrad. The young family ended up with a single room at 27 Kirovsky Prospekt: thirty square metres, divided into living and sleeping areas. It was cramped but not bleak, as 'my mother always had a housekeeper. It was always a peasant girl, usually a very simple girl who lived with us and who helped my mother with me. But my mother herself usually did all the shopping and cooking.' The block even had a doorman to act as a concierge, stack firewood in the courtyard, and do routine repairs: 'All of our guests complained about him because he would open the door for everyone and bow, and he should have been reprimanded for it.'

Heating and cooking were by wooden stove, toilets were communal, and the bath was a large tub filled with hot water brought out when needed. This may seem grim, but at least the toilet was inside: when Larissa came to live in Oxford in 1967, the house Francis bought for them had it at the bottom of the garden. He visited her in Leningrad in the spring of 1963, and left a description:

As in all the Russian flats I thereafter visit, the entrance of the building is extremely squalid … Inside the flat itself (on the 5th floor) is a small passage on to which open a number of doors; some of these belong to the 'neighbours' (ie, in fact, sharers of the flat) and some to Larissa and her mother. The kitchen and bathroom/lavatory is communal. There is no hot water except when special appliances are lit. Her section consists of one large, light dining/sitting room and one bedroom divided by a screen in two. There is a piano, some rather bad pictures, a tv set, tables, chairs etc and in one corner a huge porcelain stove reaching right up to the ceiling. (5 April 1963)

It had not always been like this, though. When the family moved in, Larissa recalled that it had been:

an incredibly luxurious apartment, and consisted of about two rooms. One was a huge hall that had two fireplaces ... I remember myself in this room, I was probably about two years old and I was always scared because it was completely impossible to heat. The fireplaces gave very little warmth and I only remember running from end to end, and it was a very long distance.

However, the flat began to shrink, as they were officially sharing with Nikolai's brother, who was away on a posting with the Baltic Fleet. When he returned, the apartment was divided into two, although with a shared entrance. Larissa loved this period – there were more people to pay attention to her, and Uncle Yevgeny's wife was an excellent baker, who plied her with buns. But when they moved out, the city allocated their portion to a total stranger, a photographer who turned into a chronic drunkard when his wife suddenly died after a botched abortion. Apart from the noise, the problem was that he would come back late at night without his keys, knocking and ringing the doorbell until someone let him in. This was at the time when the great purges were beginning, and Larissa's parents were terrified every night that the hammering on the door was not the neighbour but the NKVD, come to take Nikolai away and shoot him.

Larissa's education was eccentric even before the war broke out – she didn't go to school much until she was 8 and by the time she was 14 had only spent about three years in formal education. For the rest, her mother took care of her lessons, finding people to teach her the piano, German, French and English, and enrolling friends and family to teach her how to read, write, do arithmetic and play chess. In the summer they went to the family dacha north of Leningrad: 'you had to go by train, then it was twenty miles from the station. You could rent a horse and cart. It was in a village. There were lots of vegetables because everyone had vegetable gardens there. There wasn't any meat but you could have eggs.'

The dacha was primitive but pretty, two storeys, without running water but with a well in the garden. There was a river nearby to go swimming and fishing in, and Larissa and her mother spent much of the time cooking, picking plants for salads, and going for long walks in the summer evenings when it was daylight until nearly midnight. They stayed until the last week of August – Nikolai was almost never able to come because he was invariably on postings – then returned to Leningrad to prepare for the start of the new school year on 1 September, and the bleak Russian winter soon after.

Larissa found this idyllic, but Vera hated every moment of it, as she could see no virtue at all in a simple country life and longed for the holidays to be over so she could get back to the excitement of Leningrad. Nikolai was dutiful and somewhat introverted, she was outgoing and deeply sociable:

At one point, my mother even organised dance courses and invited a couple of professionals who taught them all new steps in foxtrots, in tango. I used to sit under the table at the time. The table was usually placed on the couch, under this table I sat and with great pleasure watched everything that was happening there … The floor was parquet and there was a place to dance. That was the life she was used to and she couldn't be without it.

There is a faded photograph of one gathering – a room dominated by a large fireplace, the table covered with bread, decanters of wine and plates of smoked fish. In comparison to the West, the main difference was the lack of material possessions: even fairly senior figures in the army, like Larissa's father, had only modest living accommodation with little in it. But Vera 'didn't mind at all. Her main thing was to be constantly entertained. As long as she surrounded herself with friends, she didn't mind anything.'

While Vera provided the stimulus, her father provided the solidity, despite long absences on postings. She loved city life, he was the opposite: 'a typical country man. Hunting was his speciality. The only thing he dreamt of was to live somewhere in the woods ...' Still, it was a relationship which mostly worked

Dinner at the Salmins, *c.* 1935

well and was almost the only marriage that Larissa knew of which did not end in divorce. He was always respectful of both wife and daughter, always responsible, and always present even when away. Both mother and daughter depended on him totally, and when he died of a heart attack in 1961 Vera had a breakdown and Larissa was heartbroken with grief. He taught her to read, took her fishing and showed her how to pick mushrooms on walks in the countryside, took her seriously and supported her: 'Every time I quarrelled with my mother, my father would be on my side and defend me. So, whenever my mother quarrelled with my father, I was always on his side.'

But Vera's self-indulgence did more to keep the family alive and safe than Nikolai's diligence. In fact, he owed his life to her insatiable craving for company and entertainment. He spent his entire career working his way up the ranks, having to overcome considerable headwinds because of his family origins. He wrote two books on chemical warfare, began to add air defence to his expertise in artillery, and as a result got his big break, recruited in January 1935 onto the staff of Marshal Mikhail Nikolaevich Tukhachevskiy, the most dynamic and influential Soviet strategic theorist of his generation. Only a few years older than Nikolai, and another graduate of the Kadetsky Korpus from a noble family, Tukhachevskiy was revered by his followers, disliked by his rivals and, unfortunately for him, seen as a dangerous potential rival by Stalin. The family travelled with Nikolai to Moscow on a posting to help reorganise the Red Army and prepare it for the war everyone knew would come sooner or later.

Nikolai dreamed of serving his country; Vera dreamed of being a general's wife; and Larissa liked being with her father. 'I remember how he got off the tram and he had such incredibly polished boots that were very shiny. And then he took me by the arm …' But there was a problem: Vera was miserable and came to

Vera Salmina, *c.* 1937 and Nikolai Salmin, *c.* 1935

hate Moscow. 'We were given a flat in the outskirts ... an awful modern building. He went to work early in the morning and my mother was left with me. I was always sick. It was hell for her.' Vera missed her friends and her city with a longing that seems common among exiled Leningraders. She wanted to go home. The army was surprisingly sympathetic – the family was offered an apartment on Gorky Street, the most prestigious in Moscow, as an incentive to stay.

But Vera could not be persuaded and became so depressed that her husband, and the Red Army, gave way. Nikolai asked to give up his post, even though he was certain that it would ruin his career. He was demoted, took a pay cut, and was transferred back to Leningrad in mid-1936, then was posted to Novgorod, where Vera and Larissa briefly joined him. 'We then had one room, which was so full of bedbugs that Dad had to put the iron bed in the middle of the room and food cans filled with kerosene around it. But, of course, that didn't help because the bedbugs were diving from the ceiling.' From there he transferred to Dubrovka, not far from Leningrad, took part in the Russian–Finnish war, and in 1940 was sent to Tbilisi in Georgia to run the Air Defence Directorate of the Caucasus.

It was wise to leave Moscow. Possibly prompted by a German disinformation campaign, Tukhachevskiy was arrested on 22 May 1937. He was tortured, to the point that his surviving confession is spattered with his blood. He was then put on trial for treason and was executed on 12 June. Subsequently, a further 37,000 officers were dismissed, more than 10,000 were arrested and more than 7,000 found guilty of crimes against the state, so weakening the Red Army it could barely hold its own even against the Finns in the 1939–40 Winter War: 'The man who had offered my mother the flat on Gorky Street was shot, along with others. All our friends were arrested.'

Tukhachevskiy's entire network of friends and colleagues – the latter carefully selected for their talent and dedication – was destroyed. He was accused of planning a *coup d'état* and of having fascist sympathies. But not Nikolai. He fully expected to be swept up in the purges sooner or later – so much so, that for a while he went to bed every night with a packed suitcase by the door; if the police came for him, he would be able to leave without disturbing his wife and daughter. But the knock never came. Perhaps his decision to leave Moscow was taken as disaffection from Tukhachevskiy's circle, perhaps his moving from posting to posting meant that he was forgotten, but he was never arrested. Although he remained in his reduced rank for a while, he otherwise emerged unscathed. There is, though, an alternative explanation for his survival. Around the time the family came back to Leningrad, a young chess player was suddenly arrested, taken away, and eventually shot when the purges were at their height. No one ever knew why, or what he was charged with. No explanation was ever given. He had no known political opinions, no dangerous friends, and seems to have lived an entirely innocuous life. His name was also Nikolai Salmin.[1]

Nikolai's brother Yevgeny was less fortunate than his younger sibling: while stationed at the naval base of Kronstadt in 1937 he was arrested and detained for a year, during which time he was continually tortured: 'He was put in such a cold ice pit and they demanded that he confess that he was the initiator of a conspiracy against Stalin. He said he would sign anything as long as it wasn't something so completely ridiculous.' How long he could have postponed execution is uncertain, but the machinations of Soviet politics came to his rescue: Nikolai Yezhov, who became head of the NKVD by arresting and shooting his predecessor, Genrikh Yagoda, was himself toppled and executed by the even more violent Lavrentiy Beria.

Beria was not noted for his sense of justice but held that anyone locked up by his predecessors was likely to be on his side. So Yevgeny Salmin was released and restored to his rank and job. He was sent back to the Baltic Fleet, where he was a specialist in mines and torpedo tactics, and stayed with it until he retired in 1954 with the official reputation of an 'experienced officer who enjoys a well-deserved authority'. On his return from prison he regaled dinner guests with tales of his torture, while the 7-year-old Larissa hid under the dining table and listened with fascination until she was discovered and shooed off to bed.

Hiding under the table seems to have been an important part of Larissa's education, as her parents frequently had visitors who would talk perfectly openly about every subject under the sun. From this practice she learned early on about the importance of knowing who could be trusted, and who needed to be treated with caution. She learned a lot about the world too. Not only did she eagerly absorb her father's and uncle's tales of military life and their very low opinions of bureaucrats and politicians, but she also listened to her mother and friends discussing the constant affairs, abortions and assorted other difficulties of their social circle.

After both of these near disasters, Vera was persuaded to leave Leningrad and join her husband in the Caucasus in 1941, just before Germany launched Operation Barbarossa in June and invaded the Soviet Union. Once more Larissa avoided going to school, and once more her mother was miserable and desperate to get back home, although Larissa herself remembered the interlude as a wonderful period. Tbilisi was a long way away but hardly barbaric: a rather beautiful city complete with opera houses, theatres and museums, it had the added benefit of being about eighty miles from the Turkish border, and a very long way from the German army. But that was still not good enough for Vera, and in summer – despite the invasion – she decided to go home with Larissa, nominally to get clothes for the winter. Nikolai reluctantly arranged the transport even though the railway network was already beginning to seize up as military needs took over more and more capacity. He insisted that they come back as soon as possible, as he was worried that Leningrad might be attacked. Vera promised, she and Larissa left, but when they arrived home, Leningrad was still peaceful. 'It was so beautiful. It was summer and there were white nights.' Vera forgot her promise and decided to stay for a while to spend more time with friends. Then for a little longer.

'Then the Germans came.'

# 2

# Francis: Background, Birth and Education, 1928–1946

*A Taxi to the Channel – Grandparents – Parents – Ignorance of England, Familiarity with France – Loathing of Prep School – Unhappiness at Eton – Anti-Semitism*

Arnold Haskell, Francis's father, was always as eager to get away from home as Larissa's mother was to return to it. Consequently, Francis was shaped by Europe, and above all by France. He was taken there nearly every year as a small boy, and one of his most vivid memories was in the late summer of 1939, when the family realised that war was about to break out because the waiter at their favourite restaurant in the Pyrenees was recalled to his regiment. As in Russia in 1941, the French train system ground to a halt, so Arnold hired a taxi to drive them the 450 miles to the English Channel, the driver grumbling all the way: 'I will become a resister. If the police try to requisition my taxi, I'll shoot them.' For the 11-year-old Francis this was so thrilling that a decade later he and some friends bought an old English taxi and drove around France in it at a steady 15 mph, recreating the great adventure of his childhood. When, finally, he was done with school and the

The taxi: Francis on the roof, the painter John Eyles by the door,
August 1950

war was over, the first thing he did was persuade his parents to let him go and live in Paris, which began a love affair with the city that never completely ended.

He believed that his was the last generation of the British whose focus was primarily on the continent, while the mentality of the generation after him was shaped overwhelmingly by the United States. His idea of America was fixed when it was isolationist, as culturally weak as it was diplomatically and militarily insignificant, with Europe being the home of Empires and the fount of all ideas of importance from literature to art and from physics to medicine. Those born a decade later knew America only as the world's greatest superpower, hoovering up the most important scientists and artists from a Europe that lay in self-imposed ruin, morally bankrupt and economically devastated. He did travel to America from the 1960s onwards – often going by ship because of his pathological fear of flying – but there is a sense in his diary entries that he could never quite take the place seriously. Certainly, it never came close to challenging the dominating influence of European culture on his outlook.

Francis's grandfather was the most interesting person in his family. Jacob Silas Haskell (so stated on his naturalisation certificate; his name may have been Eskell) was born in 1857 in Baghdad, and worked for the Sassoons, whose trading operations stretched from Egypt to China via Mesopotamia and India; he was perhaps a distant relation of that family. Based originally in Iraq, the Sassoons had spread out in multiple directions – Aleppo, Alexandria, Cairo, Athens, Bombay, Shanghai and Hong Kong. They operated in Burma and Malaya and traded in everything, establishing the banks and building the docks to meet their needs. A lucrative trade was in opium; David Sassoon had established the family as a dominant supplier of Indian opium to China and recycled the profits into other ventures. They had an astonishing ability to spot trends: they established cotton plantations in Egypt just as the American Civil War cut off supplies from the Southern states; they were among the first to realise the coming importance of oil and see that the Persian Gulf and what was then Mesopotamia would be important as a source of it; they foresaw that Cairo would expand greatly and bought up large portions of the farmland around it for development.

With near perfect timing, they saw the need for a bank in London, and Jacob Silas Haskell, who had transferred to London from Hong Kong in 1899, was given the task of setting it up. The Eastern Bank Ltd was established in 1909 with capital of £1 million (about £100 million today), much of which was provided by the Sassoons. Its initial purpose was to link domestic Indian banking with the European money markets. As *The Times* noted, foreign exchange business was run by the three great Presidency

Banks of Calcutta, Bombay and Madras, but these had little to do with what it termed 'country bankers'. Eastern would link the two sectors: 'Shipments to and from India and the East will be financed … while a further large scope will be found for the profitable employment of money by making advances to natives and Europeans against merchandise and other securities.' Essentially, it planned to raise money in London at low rates of interest and lend it out in India, where rates were much higher, to fund trade from which the Sassoons could profit still further. It continued, however, to finance the opium business – in 1913 the chairman apologised to shareholders for a lowered dividend as the Chinese were cheating and growing their own.

Eastern Banker: Mr J. S. Haskell

Eastern was rapidly successful; with Sassoon money, the expertise of people like Jacob Silas and the addition of City luminaries such as Lord Balfour as chairman for the first few years, it swiftly became profitable. In the first year, it made a profit of £23,000. This near doubled to £55,000 in 1911, then £122,000 by 1920, by which time it had expanded to Karachi, and opened branches in Baghdad and Basra after Britain's acquisition of the region. By then, Jacob Silas had become chairman, a post he occupied until his death in 1938. He also sat on the Iraqi Currency Board, which oversaw the country's monetary policy from London. With a Sassoon – Sir Sassoon Eskell – as Minister of Finance in Baghdad, and Jacob Silas in London looking after the currency, the family all but controlled the entire country, and ran its finances so well that Iraq had the most solid economy in the region for decades afterwards, with unmatched social services until they were finally destroyed in 2003.[1]

Francis talked little of his grandfather, beyond mentioning that he was always oddly afraid of running out of money. His own father, Arnold, was only slightly more forthcoming:

> I was an only child, my father was wealthy, my mother artistic … My father, who was years older than my mother, took not the slightest interest in any form of art … my mother, on the contrary, did her utmost to educate me … He was ultra-conservative, I was therefore very much to the left. He was a banker, I affected to despise all business. He refrained from pointing out … that all my artistic experiences were subsidized by his banking.[2]

Jacob Silas was Jewish, and had taken British citizenship in 1900. In 1901, at the age of 44, he married Emilie Mesritz, of a Jewish family in Arnhem. She was 20, and came from an equally commercial background: her father was an accountant, her grand-father a factory manager. Arnold, their only child, was born two years later. Thereafter, the family set to work assimilating into London as well as foreign Jews could at the time. Emmy – an assiduous collector of autographs in her youth – became a noted patroness of the arts, particularly ballet, as well as a fairly competent sculptor; Jacob Silas joined clubs and read *The Times*. They seem to have downplayed their Judaism; while both were buried in Jewish cemeteries, neither appears to have taken any role in Jewish society in England. Their son Arnold went still further; he wrote two volumes of autobiography and did not refer to his religion in either, except when talking about his conversion to Catholicism without ever mentioning what he was converting from.[3]

Arnold was certainly very different to both his father and his son; he was a dilettante who never felt any urge to settle down to any orthodox career, and who was confident in the knowledge that he would never need to. He went to Westminster School and to Cambridge, which he left without a degree, then worked as a publisher's assistant until he developed an interest in ballet. Thereafter, he devoted his life to the subject, although never to the point of earning much of a living from it. Nonetheless, his efforts did popularise dance in Britain and Australia, and he became a foremost critic and commentator, to the point that he ended up being influential in the development of ballet education and – crucially – formed contacts in the Soviet Union, the country so obsessed with and important for ballet that even English dancers felt compelled to adopt Russian stage names in homage. Thus the dancer Lilian Marks, discovered by Emmy and developed and supported by Arnold, changed her name to Alicia Markova in order to be taken seriously.[4]

Francis's parents were in their different ways demand-ing, controlling and frightening. Despite his father's two autobiographies, it is difficult to get a real sense of Arnold. His self-presentation was as a charming, intelligent connoisseur of the arts, a pioneer familiar with the great and the good in the artistic world. But he was also desperately vain – in his first memoir he informs the reader within the first three pages that he had a photographic memory, spoke fluent French by the age of 4, possessed the gift of making friends easily and had been awarded the *Légion d'honneur*. Arnold was happy to live off his own father's wealth, but did not extend the same favour to his children. Francis and his siblings inherited some money from their grandfather but found their own parents to be rather parsimonious. Arnold's own needs for money trumped those of his children.

While Francis's mother took him to museums and art galleries, Arnold would sit the young boy down, quiz him on current affairs, and hand him photographs of paintings, demanding to know who painted them, whether they were good or not, how they related to other paintings. Francis found these interrogations terrifying:

I sometimes wonder whether this obsessive anxiety to know things ... doesn't spring from the humiliations of the General Knowledge Tests that Daddy used to give me when a boy – just as my present career may spring from the fact that on one of those occasions ... I couldn't name three paintings and their artists. (19 August 1962)

His father was often not there – he travelled with ballet companies around Europe, the US and even to Australia, so his presence was felt only when his return coincided with school holidays. When he was at home his opinions ruled and, while he liked to think of himself as tolerant and generous, his eldest child did not see him that way. Francis's diaries record many arguments, expressions of disdain and inadequacy, to the point that he later acknowledged the family 'did not work very well'. He retained relations with his parents – not least because his father responded so well to his desire to get married – but his brother had a break- down and his sister, the youngest, ended up living in New York, far away from family.

The general ambience was made still more continental in outlook because Arnold married the daughter of Ukrainian émigrés in Paris. Curiously, the way he met his wife followed

The Haskell family, Paris, 1946
(*left to right*: Stephen, Helen, Arnold, Vera, Francis)

exactly the same pattern as that of Francis nearly four decades later: 'The minute I set eyes on her I knew I was going to marry her ... As soon as I proposed she asked my advice, and I told her she had better accept.'[5] The woman he married, Vera Markovna Zaitseva, came from a formerly very wealthy Jewish family which had controlled the sugar industry in Kiev before the Revolution. Her sister Tatyana married a cousin, the novelist Mark Aldanov (born Landau). The entire family left Ukraine after the Revolution and travelled via Constantinople, Berlin and Brussels before settling in France, losing all the businesses, property and money in the process. Thereafter, they lived a bohemian and impecunious life among the large community of Russian émigrés in Paris – among them Larissa's own grandfather – until the Second World War broke out and they had to flee again, this time to the United States.

Of Francis's mother, there is little that can be said: she rarely figures in his diaries, except for the occasional complaint about her nosiness and tendency to give him unwanted advice. There are more references to her family in France than there are to her. Once the campaign to marry and extract Larissa got under way, there are several letters from her, but these are oddly distant – hoping he is well, but showing no further interest. Rather, they are overwhelmingly concerned with telling him about concerts seen, places visited, and people met: she was assiduous in keeping in contact, but mainly preoccupied with herself. Perhaps this is unfair: the reputations of few parents could easily survive the gaze of an adolescent, certainly not one with a diary and a gift for words. But Larissa didn't like her much either: 'She was incredibly bossy ... I found it totally unbearable. The last thing I wanted was to tell her anything.'

Nor did Francis's father have much to say about her, beyond conventional remarks about how she had provided 'an ideal home life'. In his first autobiography she is scarcely mentioned at all; in the second she is mentioned three times, and her death gets four paragraphs, most of which concern Arnold's reaction and her effect on his work. Of her character, her personality, there is almost nothing. This provides a clue for Francis's own life: it is difficult not to conclude that he was searching for a relationship which was the exact opposite of the one his parents had created.

It would be wrong to write off her influence too quickly, however. Vera added a great deal of the cosmopolitanism to Francis's life, as well as normalising the idea of marrying a Russian, even though he never learned the language. Thus, as a child, he remembered Vladimir Nabokov coming to talk to him in his bedroom when the novelist was visiting – author and infant shared an interest in butterflies; Francis slipped into the circles of often down at heel Russians when he went to Paris; and above all he got to know Aldanov, Uncle Max, as the Zaitsevs returned to France as quickly as possible once Paris was liberated in August 1944.

As Arnold spoke little Russian, and his wife only imperfect English, Francis was born on 7 April 1928 into a French-speaking household, and that was his first language. Combined with an initial schooling at the Lycée Française in Kensington, his focus was always over the English Channel. Being sent as a boarder to English schools at the age of 8, and then confined to England for the duration of the war and afterwards for National Service, was experienced as the worst form of imprisonment: 'The government has banned all foreign travel, but I will get abroad somehow, for I MUST' (6 April 1947).

The war itself had little impact on his life until his parents' house in Hornton Street, South Kensington, was hit by a V1 bomb on 4 July 1944. No one was injured, although much of his father's art collection was destroyed in the blaze. But the loss was not so traumatic that it warranted a mention in the diaries Francis had recently begun to write, and for the most part his life progressed much as it would have done in peace time. His prep school was evacuated to Gloucestershire for a while, but by the time he began at Eton, the government was giving up on evacuating children from cities as counterproductive. Eton was far too influential to be requisitioned by the military as many others were, and the privations and shortages of war were hardly noticeable. The school had always taken a somewhat Spartan approach to its pupils – no heating, little hot water, and scarcely edible food – so fuel shortages and rationing made scant difference. Francis's main concern was that the war would last so long that he might end up having to fight in it, but by 1944 the end was in sight, and by then he realised he was going to be drafted anyway. So he focused instead on learning the art of survival in a hostile environment. He had been miserable at his prep school, to which he was sent away as a boarder at the age of 8, and for the first three years he hated Eton even more.

This was inevitable. The school was an institution dedicated to producing a ruling caste and did not value intellectuality overmuch – 'its boys are not chosen for their intelligence ...'[6] Francis had none of the qualities of the natural leader of men, was not in the slightest bit interested in sports, and had little in common with most of his fellow pupils. They came from the ranks of the aristocracy, the landed gentry, politics or the professions, while he was the grandson of an Iraqi Jew and the son of a dilettante ballet critic. But eventually he made enough friends to make life tolerable, and in the last year was almost happy, although depression and fear were never far beneath the surface.

Apart from the normal miseries of school life, the whole period was blighted by his first experience of anti-Semitism. While at prep school near Margate his nominal religion had mattered little and he was brought up in an entirely secular environment, knowing far more about Christianity than he did about Judaism. But Eton, where he went in September 1941, was different and the experience marked him deeply, his fears re-emerging unpredictably in the decades that followed. On VE Day, 8 May 1945, for example, the whole school erupted with singing, drinking and festivities to celebrate: 'At 10.15 we went out to see the bonfire lit on Fellow's Eyot. It was a wonderful sight and there were also some fireworks. The mob spirit, however, rather spoiled things, because several people were thrown in the river, and I was frightened there would be a "Jews!" cry ...'

He had reason to be afraid, as periodically the sportier variety of pupil would go on a Jew hunt, taunting them and throwing them into the Thames. In about 1949, when he was 21, he wrote a separate account of this period:

I had never come across anti-Semitism before, and it came as a shock. I suffered terribly, and if I came across anything approaching such sentiments, the whole of the rest of my day could be ruined. What's more, I suffered in silence ... Before then, being a Jew hadn't made any difference, except that I was regarded as rather lucky at Prep School because I didn't have to study the New Testament. That was all. Now, suddenly, it seemed that I was something apart, and inferior to the other members of the school ... If anyone was good to me, I was exaggeratedly grateful ... Although I didn't show it much, that did make me extremely miserable and left rather a deep impression. However, as I and my companions grew older, this gradually stopped, and, externally at any rate, my last two years at Eton were glorious. I had success, I joined societies, things went well, and by the time I was in the Sixth Form, I was really beginning to conquer my inferiority complex, largely brought about by my early encounter with anti-Semitism. Externally. But internally things were different. I had moods from time to time of terrible depression ... During these moods – of course, they are frequent among Jews – I used to reach a state of complete despair, not only about my own life, but about the world in general. I used to contemplate suicide, almost seriously, and feel I had to escape my present existence at all costs.

The fear returned once more when he was doing his National Service in 1946–8. Exposed for the first time in his life to the mass of his fellow countrymen, he was completely horrified by the experience, but was above all terrified that someone might realise he was Jewish. Although it was only a short while since the revelations about the concentration camps, it was nonetheless a period of heightened anti-Semitism in Britain, especially in the army. Having narrowly escaped the dangers of fighting against Germany, many of his fellow conscripts were outraged at the idea that they might instead be shipped off to Palestine and what they considered somebody else's civil war. The growing incidence of terrorist attacks by groups like the Irgun, such as the bombing of the headquarters of the British armed forces at the King David Hotel in Jerusalem a few months before Francis was called up, did not help either: however sympathetic they may have been as details of the Holocaust emerged, few conscripts felt indulgent to those who wished to kill them. Francis did not fear being sent to Palestine himself – the army quickly recognised that he had no military aptitude whatsoever – but he did fear those who might be:

On my first day in the army, I registered myself as Church of England and not Jewish ... I didn't have the courage to admit that I was a Jew ... How many times ... did I listen to the news reader announcing further deaths in Jerusalem and Tel Aviv and hear the comments 'Dirty Yids,' 'They should kill the lot' and so on ... I did not really resent the attitude of the troops, for it was an attitude which was perfectly understandable and was encouraged by the politicians and newspapers ... No-one knew that I was a Jew, and I was treated for what I was. People didn't judge me, as at Eton ...

# 3

# Larissa: Siege, Evacuation, Return, 1941–1944

*Bombs, Sugar and Perfume – A Frozen Grandmother –*
*Eating a Horse – Cooking a Cat – Picking Vegetables in*
*No-Man's Land – Rotten Sardines – The Road of Life – Train*
*Ride to Ufa – Spanish Revolutionaries – Rabies – Stalingrad –*
*Return to Moscow – Fields of Corpses – Going Feral*

While Francis was beginning his new life at Eton in September 1941, Larissa was stuck in a city about to endure the most violent and destructive event in modern history, with a death toll far exceeding that of Hiroshima and Nagasaki combined. The siege of Leningrad began on 8 September and lasted until 27 January 1944, a total of 872 days. The number killed was gigantic, the suffering even greater. Up to 1.5 million civilians and soldiers died, many from starvation or hypothermia. This was a deliberate policy to ensure that 'Leningrad must die of starvation'. Once it was clear the city was not going to surrender, the German army did not wish to waste its resources through a frontal assault. But the ultimate goal was clear: 'St Petersburg must be erased from the face of the Earth ... we have no interest in saving lives of the civilian population.'[1] The underlying assumption was that a tight blockade would accomplish German aims within a few weeks. The Russians were unprepared and had evacuated few people before the siege began; the city received little outside assistance until November, and thereafter supplies in, and evacuations out, were patchy, very dangerous and always inadequate.

The siege was a deliberate act of attempted genocide with the damage and casualties far exceeding any comparable military operation of the war. The 11-year-old Larissa was in the middle of it – literally so, as she lived near the centre of the city. She was fortunate, as the outskirts suffered the most. Her experience of the siege, and her memories, were impressionistic. Uppermost were sensations – cold, hunger and, above all, smell; in order to hurry the process of starvation along, the Germans deliberately shelled food stores, and early in the siege hit warehouses stocked with sugar, which then burned to the ground. When sugar burns it produces a hideous and unforgettable smell; eighty years later, the particular, indescribable stink covering the whole of the city remained prominent in her recollections. Another, stranger, aroma challenged this memory. Cars vanished from the streets very swiftly as there was no petrol to spare for any except military vehicles. But at one stage people realised that oils used to manufacture scent could be used instead and stole as much as they could: 'Cars drove by on perfume oils, from perfume factories. Therefore, when a car passed, there was such an incredible, wonderful aroma. I remember that very well.'

But the siege seems to have produced no long-lasting emotional trauma; Larissa's account of so many years later contained no reference to fear, anxiety and certainly not happiness or pleasure. Rather, it seems that all the emotions were tamped down; the desire to live was so strong, and the business of survival so all-consuming, that there was no energy to waste on emotions; instead, a steady doggedness, a determination to get through every day, swamped all else.

Besides, 11-year-olds are in no position to take decisions and, while Vera was in some ways scatty and frivolous, she was also devoted, ingenious and very determined. As long as she was there, Larissa felt looked after and safe. Certainly, survival required imagination and daring, an ability to spot an opportunity and grab hold of it before someone else did.

> The bombs started to fall and soon after that our rations were minimal. We all received 120 grams of bread but the bread consisted of hay and sand so there was little flour in it. We became very hungry but fortunately the shop was very close to us, and it opened at six o'clock in the morning. When I read memoirs they say how extremely difficult it was to get bread, but our small shop next door to us was always open and deserted.

Above all, there was the everyday, random violence, so omni-present that it became normal and almost accepted:

> And, of course, a huge number of corpses were all around. There were corpses lying on our stairs, we had to pass by without looking at them. There were corpses lying in the courtyard. There were men lying and women lying dead. So we've seen it all, but we developed a kind of immunity to all of this. It seemed completely normal … on the contrary, it somehow seemed fun … the fact is that all these memories we have, oddly enough, are quite bright, not in any way tragic.

This did not mean that Larissa was unaffected by events: even if she was protected and much had taken place in the background, by the age of 11 she had lived through the disappearance of her uncle and tales of his torture; had moved around from place to place after her father; felt her parents' anxiety about the possibility of being caught up in the purges; and then had to endure the horrors of the siege. All of this had an impact, even if no one seems to have made the connection when she didn't want to do her piano practice: 'I remember taking two bricks and putting a finger on one and breaking it with the other ... Then I started screaming wildly ...' Another time, 'I pierced my cheek with scissors; I had this tendency to mutilate myself somehow as a child.' She also set fire to the apartment: 'I don't remember where I got the matches but I lit a pretty big fire. I had to put it out somehow, and I pulled out a rather large suitcase from under the bed to smother it but the suitcase caught fire too ...'

The meagre rations they were allowed were jealously guarded, and never shared: 'You would think that mothers would give their children more but they didn't. We cut the food up evenly and ate it within a second.' Any subterfuge which presented itself was eagerly grasped. Larissa's best friend at the Hermitage, Marta Kryzhanovskaya, was sent to live with her grandmother nearby, but while she was there in the middle of winter, the old woman died. The neighbours immediately rolled her body in a blanket and put it on the balcony, where it froze solid. Marta had to live with her grandmother's corpse just outside the window, but she got to claim and eat the old woman's food allowance.[2]

Official rations were nowhere near enough and the entire population was on the lookout for anything else they might eat to stay alive. When her mother was walking along a street one day, a horse slipped on the snow and was too exhausted to get up again. 'The horse was still alive but a crowd of people ran

Marta Kryzhanovskaya, *c.* 1955

to tear it apart with their hands. The horse cried whilst it was pulled to pieces.' Vera got hold of a chunk which fed them for days. Larissa's grandmother worked in a clothes factory which used buttons made from antlers. She would steal these and boil them on the stove – when there was fuel – and they produced just enough watery nutrition to make a small difference. Larissa could remember having a button in her mouth, sucking it for hours, pretending it was proper food.

And they ate the cats. First her grandmother's, which Vera slaughtered and roasted, then the next door neighbour's:

It was a snow-white Persian cat, of incredible beauty and the owner did not want to give it up. And, lo and behold, on some very gloomy day, my mother went up the stairs and saw that the cat was running and screaming from hunger … Well, we took it and my mother stabbed it and we ate it. But it was only skin and bone because it was very emaciated.

This one they had to boil up for soup as it was so skinny, but Larissa got to gnaw on the tail and found it particularly tasty. Curiously, the population of Leningrad did not eat the zoo, as Parisians had done during the German siege of 1870–1. The keepers – a bit more prescient than most – had evacuated most of the animals before the siege began, and then fiercely protected those elephants, vultures and hippos which remained.[3]

Weeds were equally sought after. Leningrad itself was densely built up and all vegetable matter was rapidly stripped and eaten, but the family benefitted once more from army connections, particularly Nikolai's friendship with Vladislav Rostislavóvich Tregubov, a colonel he had known for years, who also came from an old noble background. Tregubov was chief of staff of the Leningrad air defences and promised to do his best to keep his eye on Nikolai's family when they came back from Tbilisi. So, occasionally, he lent them his staff car and a driver: 'This took us through the lines onto fields between our troops and the Germans. There were lots of bits of rotten cabbage. My mother would dig them up and cook them. That was delicious.' Finally Vera's friend Jadviga Mikhailova – who moved in with her son Yura shortly after the siege began – paid her way in food:

She was a very beautiful woman, very cold and very beautiful. Her husband was at the front, and she had a lot of admirers. We were sitting and starving and suddenly the

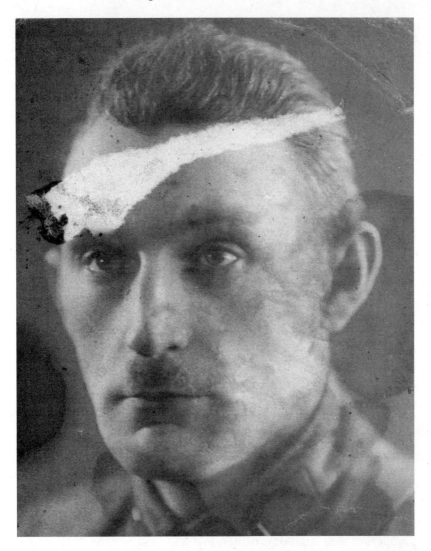

Vladislav Rostislavovich Tregubov

bell rings. The door opens and a bag of potatoes rolls in. It turns out that one of her admirers was carrying seed potatoes somewhere and decided to give them to her. He could have been shot on the spot for such theft, and yet he was ready for the sake of this beloved woman to do anything.

Jadviga Mikhailova

Another admirer was the commander of a ship in the Baltic Fleet, who chose to woo her with cans of rotting fish dredged up from sunken ships in Kronstadt harbour. 'He would take her hands and recite poetry to her. All she could think about was when he would leave so she could eat. If anyone ate that now, they would probably die … but strangely, all stomach illnesses disappeared during that time. Whatever you ate, you never got poisoned.'

Getting washed was a special torment, particularly because of the desire for respectability underlying it:

What if a person was very dirty and died the next day? So they washed us continuously, just in case. It was a terrible torture. They put a tub next to the stove, brought water from Leo Tolstoy Square, quite far away, which they carried in buckets, heated it on this stove with driftwood and scrubbed until we were clean.

This even continued when Vera ran out of soap: rather than tolerating a little dirt, she scraped her daughter clean with 'ashes and mustard' instead. Larissa found this to be even worse.

During this period Larissa fell in love with Shakespeare, not because of the beauty of the poetry or the quality of the stories, but because he is one of the few writers who almost never mentions eating: 'We couldn't read Chekhov or Tolstoy because they all wrote about food.' She would wrap herself up as warmly as possible and read for hours without being reminded of how hungry she was. And they went to the cinema when the electricity was on: 'We watched pre-war films. It seemed so utterly unrealistic. The cinema wasn't heated but the blue light from the screen gave the illusion of warmth. It was minus twenty but for an hour or so we didn't feel it.'

Initially there was considerable fear about the bombings; German aircraft came over regularly and could do great damage even if they missed their target. For the previous decade, in Russia as well as the West more generally, belief in the destructive power of bombers had been firmly ingrained. In England many believed that the Luftwaffe was capable of flattening an entire city in a matter of days, with the 1937 attack on Guernica in Spain – badly damaged in the first mass air-raid in history – cited as the main evidence.

These fears, although very far from imaginary, were overblown at the time, but until the German military settled on the strategy of starving everyone to death rather than killing them directly, there were many attacks, and initially Vera took all possible precautions – their friend Tregubov rang her up to warn her when he heard of an incoming raid. On multiple occasions in the first weeks, she led Larissa and the others into the basement and stayed there for hours. But after a week or so, she began to get bored: 'She was too lazy. She decided that if a bomb hit our house we would die anyway. So we stopped going.' Larissa was more cautious – if a warning sounded when she was out and about alone, she would dive into the snowdrifts piled up when the streets were cleared, even though these provided little real protection and it was dangerous to stay covered too long. When spring came in 1942, hundreds of bodies of people who had taken similar refuge and frozen to death emerged from the melting drifts.

There were also moments of strange and surreal beauty:

What I still remember very well before our departure is the wild fires ... a whole building caught fire very easily and it could not be extinguished because it was more than 20 degrees below zero, even 30 degrees, and the water in the hose pipes immediately froze. That's why some houses burned. One on Kirovsky Prospekt caught fire and it was very beautiful. The frosty air, the snow all around, the flames, and the whole building burning ...

And so the winter went on, with Vera using all her skills and cunning to ensure that they had enough food to keep going, and enough warmth to avoid freezing. They burned in the stove any piece of wood they could find in the streets and then most of their furniture, but Larissa was grateful that the family library was spared, as careful experiment demonstrated that books were hard to light and did not give off much heat.

In early March 1942, after six months of siege, they got the chance to escape. The government was organising convoys of trucks and buses which headed around the north of the German lines by going over the frozen Lake Ladoga to a still-operational railway. It was a slow trip – the shortest route was sixteen miles over the ice, the longest more than sixty – and exceptionally dangerous. Continually falling snow meant that vehicles could easily get stuck; the Germans knew exactly where the route was and frequently shelled it – an explosion on a crust of ice over water could cause havoc, even when the ice was five feet thick. There was little lighting and trucks got lost easily, especially because nearly all of the trips took place at night. Moreover, the convoys were irregular – the cold meant that supplies of petrol were erratic, the vehicles broke down or froze, and in any case there weren't enough of them. Saving people was not the main priority – the initial purpose was to ferry supplies of weaponry and food in, and then extract industrial equipment and some artistic treasures, but from late January the decision was taken to evacuate as many as possible, beginning with children. Between then and the beginning of April, when warming temperatures made the route too dangerous for anything but light trucks, more than half a million civilians were taken out of the city.

Larissa and her mother were among the earliest. Quite how their escape was organised she could not remember, although it is likely that their guardian angel Tregubov had a hand in the matter once more. Certainly, when they left, they departed in a small van which was sent to pick them up at their apartment, hardly the normal arrangement. But it was Vera who ensured that Jadviga and her son came out at the same time; her friend said that she would otherwise kill herself. Only family groups were permitted to go, so Vera solved the problem by the simple expedient of writing the permissions herself and forging documents to show that

Jadviga was her sister. These would not have survived careful scrutiny, but there was no time for anyone to give the papers much attention. All four got into the back of the van and they set off.

Larissa remembered the trip as the most terrifying moment of her life: 'There were trucks with weapons going down it the whole time and Germans were constantly bombing it. We would see trucks sinking under the ice but we just continued … Soldiers stood there and directed them.' The sixteen-mile trip over the ice took almost as many hours: there were so many halts, and detours around shell holes, with the constant possibility that the driver would lose his bearings when they left the marked strip cleared of snow which counted as the road.

This was only the first part, however. When the convoy got to the eastern side of the lake, it then had to drive a further twenty-five miles across the peninsula to Novaya Ladoga, the first point where there was a railway that had not been destroyed. At no point in the journey were they more than half a dozen miles from German artillery positions, which did their utmost to hit anything moving. From leaving Leningrad to arriving at the train station took more than twenty-four hours, and there was no food for the already starving refugees throughout that time, apart from the tiny amounts they had brought with them, which was soon eaten. 'When we reached the end, we were close to starvation.'

Nor was there any provided on the next stage, the train which headed slowly east. The refugees were loaded onto cattle trucks and headed off for an unknown destination. They spent more than a fortnight travelling slowly, with little food or water: 'Whenever we stopped, people would ask if there were any dead bodies. Those who had died were simply taken off and the train continued on its way.' A little food was found, exchanged for vodka or soap, but nowhere near enough, and they only managed to buy something about once a week: 'The whole train was dying. All

those who came over the Road of Life, they all died on the train.'
Larissa never found out where it was supposed to be going, all
she remembered was that eventually her 'mother realised that we
would die if we didn't get food so we got off at the next station'.
This was at Kurgan, some 1,200 miles east of Leningrad.

The whole episode was a demonstration of Vera's remarkable resourcefulness, which existed alongside her tendency to be
wayward and self-indulgent. The official evacuation was a catastrophe, and wherever they were going was unlikely to be pleasant. So
Vera – almost alone of all the evacuees, who continued to trust
that the government knew what it was doing – set off on her own,
making it up as she went. It was difficult enough to travel in the
Soviet Union at the best of times; journeying in the middle of a
war without permission was even more so, and they succeeded
only because of her ability to charm officials, and to talk her way
out of awkward situations. It wasn't simply that she wanted to get
to safety, wherever that might be found. She particularly wanted
to go to Ufa in the Urals, because a friend of hers was already
there and she needed a bit of company. This made the journey
even more complicated, but she managed it:

trains passed there but … they didn't let us on. In the end
we got on one, and eventually changed, I no longer remember where, to a real passenger compartment train … by then
I hadn't eaten a crumb for twenty four hours. In the next
compartment were some pilots who immediately started
flirting with her. They asked if I wanted a chocolate. My
mother said I could take it so I did and divided it between
all four of us.

When they arrived at Ufa they went straight to the flat taken by the parents of Larissa's friend Maya Bilikina, where they could eat, sleep and begin to relax. The Bilikin family had been evacuated early because Maya's father was an engineer and the factory where he worked was dismantled and moved the moment the war started.[4] Larissa finally gave way to the terrors of the whole episode, curled herself up tightly under a chair, and stayed there for two days, refusing to come out.

For the next eighteen months, they lived in safety in the capital of Bashkiria. Ufa started the war as a fairly small but handsome town, founded in the sixteenth century and with a mixed population of Russians, Bashkirs and Tatars. But it was expanding rapidly as both industry and people were evacuated from western Russia and from Ukraine. In addition to Russians like the Salmins, the government had packed all the exiled Spanish revolutionaries off to the town as well, and many were staying in the Hotel Bashkiria, where Vera soon found a room – supposedly only temporarily, but in fact they lived there throughout their stay. The Bashkiria was then the best hotel in the city, so new it wasn't even completed when the war began, and construction stopped before the roof was finished. But it was habitable, although the only room available was tiny:

The four of us were in a single room, my mother, Jadia, Yura and me. There were two beds and there were chairs next to the beds. I slept on the chairs. But we did have a place to wash so it was much more comfortable than living in someone else's house.

The room was expensive but the four shared it until Jadia heard her husband had been killed at the front. She left soon after to join yet another admirer, in Siberia, which meant that for the first time since they left Leningrad, Larissa was able to sleep in a proper bed.

There was at least no shortage of money. Vera had her husband's salary and quickly found a job working in a food shop, which gave her both an income and ample access to food. This position was arranged by the local, rather harried, NKVD officer, who found himself having to organise the arrival of evacuees. Vera turned on the charm again, and discovered that the officer was, like her, from Leningrad, so they struck up a connection. Besides, they were among the earliest arrivals, so placing them was not as difficult as it later became. He used his influence to get her the work in the shop, and also arranged a position as a bookkeeper for Jadia.

And so they settled in, with a job, an income and somewhere to live, the combination allowing them to have a life as close to that of Leningrad as possible. The climate was not nearly as harsh, and food was plentiful because of a thriving black market, as official-dom allowed peasants from the region to come in and sell their produce at grossly inflated prices. There was a theatre, concert hall and libraries, and Larissa went to the ballet and to operas as often as she could, as both the Kirov Ballet and Opera were relocated to the city from Leningrad and put on regular performances. Vera, of course, began to get bored but even she could see the wisdom of staying put for a while, and she made enough friends to keep her entertained, particularly Dolores Ibárruri, La Pasionaria – she of the clarion call 'No pasarán!' used to rally the republicans against Franco in the Spanish Civil War. Ibárruri was known – and feared – for her revolutionary zeal and steely discipline but Larissa found her to be quite kindly and sweet. She and the whole executive committee of the Communist International had been shipped off when Moscow came under attack – 'they went under Russian pseudonyms but everybody knew who was who' – and the Spanish contingent spent its time broadcasting encouragement back home through Radio España Independiente.[5]

Another friend was the wife of Andrei Grechko, who was also living in the same hotel. Grechko was of the same generation as Nikolai Salmin, but was rather more successful in his career, ending up as Minister of Defence under Brezhnev. Vera therefore had much in common with his wife, Claudia, and Larissa grew equally close to his daughter Tatyana. She was finally sent to school with all the Spanish children, who she discovered had a similar approach to education as she had: 'They were such fun; they never did any work at all ...' In addition, Vera organised English lessons and piano lessons, and in any case Larissa was by now such a voracious reader that she needed little formal education.

But a permanent worry was her father, who had been sent to Crimea to command an artillery regiment throughout the Battle of the Kerch Peninsula. This engagement began in December 1941, while Larissa was still in Leningrad, and went on until the following May, by which time she was in Ufa. It was one of the worst defeats that the Soviet Union suffered throughout the war, with losses of more than half a million men compared to German losses of fewer than 40,000. The Soviet army in Crimea was outmanoeuvred, outgeneralled and utterly destroyed. The Germans' aim was to capture Sevastopol, which they did in July 1942, and to prepare the ground for an all-out assault on the Caucasus mountains and their oilfields, as Germany was critically short of oil. The campaign succeeded in Crimea, but the subsequent advance on the Caucasus proved to be the turning point of the war when the lunge for the oilfields failed. Despite losses of around 1.2 million men, the Red Army fought the Germans to a standstill and ultimately began to push them back. Nikolai was sent into the Kerch Peninsula with his regiment, but he managed to escape when it was destroyed. He was demoted because of the failure, but others suffered a far greater punishment. His general, who commandeered one of the few remaining aircraft and flew to safety in Siberia, was promptly arrested for treason and desertion. Besides, Nikolai's demotion was only temporary: it was clear that the German advance was not yet finished, and that the attack on the Caucasus would start soon enough. He was recalled to Moscow to help rebuild the army for the next round.

By June 1942, Larissa's mother could stand the limited amusements of Ufa and the discomfort of living in a tiny room in the Hotel Bashkiria no more and decided that she had to move to somewhere more interesting. Nikolai had kept on the apartment in Tbilisi when he was sent to Crimea, and on the advice of the Spaniards, she booked places on a steamer down the Volga, and then on the train to Georgia. It was going to be a long journey – nearly 1,200 miles – and considering what the Germans were planning, it was an unwise choice. But it is unlikely she would ever have got there; she wanted a renewed taste of big city life to boost her spirits and thought that a stopover somewhere

Nikolai (*second from the left*) in Crimea, 1942

interesting would revive her spirits. She decided that Stalingrad would be just the place.

A week or so before they left, however, Vera was bitten by a dog badly enough to see a doctor, and he insisted that she was given a course of thirty rabies shots, in case the beast had the disease. The injections were then given directly into the stomach every day for a month and, apart from being incredibly painful, meant that travel was impossible. By the time she had the all-clear, the steamer was long gone, and the prospect of getting anywhere near their destination had evaporated as well. But for the dog, Larissa would have become one of the few people to have been in two of the bloodiest events in modern history, as the five-month-long Battle of Stalingrad which began in mid-July rivalled the siege of Leningrad for its violence and exceeded it for savagery.

So they remained in Ufa for another year. When Nikolai arrived in Moscow he was given command of the newly forming 35th Anti-Aircraft Artillery Division with instructions to make it ready for combat. He assumed command in July 1943 and once he had settled down, decided it was a good moment to recover his family. Getting hold of the travel permits proved impossible, however, as spaces were reserved solely for military purposes.

He issued a permit for a soldier of his new division to come to Moscow, saying he was vital for constructing the new fighting unit, and sent it to his wife. Vera cut her hair, dressed herself in a soldier's uniform, and set off. This was fairly risky; the war was going badly, and the number of soldiers deserting was growing; the security police monitored every train and carried out frequent checks on all passengers. Vera – who made an unconvincing soldier and had a 12-year-old girl in tow – stood out. A security man noticed her, asked for her papers, and questioned her closely. He wanted to know the soldier's name, regiment, reasons for travel. Whose was the child? Who issued the orders? It was perfectly clear he did not believe a word she said, and equally clear that he understood precisely what was going on. 'He looked at all the documents, and then shrugged and shook her hand: "Okay," he said, "go. Just don't take me for an idiot!"' As so often, the refusal of Russians, even those in the security services, to obey their own rules saved the day.

The problem was that, while Larissa's father had sent along the paperwork for train travel, he was unable to get hold of the documents needed to enter Moscow. As a result, mother and daughter got off the train at a small village outside the city and phoned his headquarters. They were given a place to meet in some woods and Nikolai commandeered a staff car and came to find them. Vera changed into ordinary clothes, burned and buried both the uniform and the travel papers, and then Nikolai drove them back to his camp, where they remained until he was dispatched to the front a few weeks later and they were allowed to move into Moscow.

They stayed there for nearly a year, living with friends in the centre of the city:

> I had a very jolly time. We lived with a very famous historian. He had a big flat and was a friend from before the war but my mother said that he acted awfully during the purges. He denounced everyone but survived. He had a very kind wife, which is why we could sleep on a sofa in the living room. He had so many books that it was paradise for me. There was me and my mother. His nephew, grandmother and daughter and her husband were also there. It was a very crowded flat and I was very friendly with Roma who was my age. I went to school in the very centre of Moscow and that was the best school I've ever been to. I was taught German by a real German. We had free breakfast there and a fantastic headteacher. It was the most wonderful time.

Despite all this, homesickness drove Vera and Larissa to make the still perilous return journey to Leningrad in early 1944. The siege was not yet fully over, but the route was open and army contacts organised the permits for one of the first trains to take civilians back to the city. It was a hideous experience, one which stuck most firmly in Larissa's memory, and one of the few with no humour about it at all:

It was impossible to look out of the windows because there were corpses lying everywhere in the fields. On both sides. Solid fields of corpses. German, ours. For mile after mile. There was not a single house and not a single tree left between Moscow and Leningrad. It was impossible to look at.

They returned to find that the building containing their apartment had been hit by a shell and damaged ('but only a little bit'); the apartment had little furniture, as that had been burned before they left, and Leningrad was eerily quiet: 'From the Moskovsky railway station to our house, we did not meet a single person and not a single car. It was a completely empty city.' In addition, their home had been turned into a virtual storeroom, 'covered from floor to ceiling with packages'.

All our friends who went to the front, went somewhere, brought everything they had and they left it in our apartment. Many of them never returned, but gradually it all disappeared. But for a while we only had a narrow passage from the dining room to the bedroom, where we could sleep and then get out of the door.

Rationing was still in force and all around there was debris from destroyed buildings. A week after they returned, Vera was drafted to work in a hospital, work so hard she had to stay and sleep there, returning only at weekends and not always then. The 13-year-old Larissa was left to fend for herself in the broken and deserted city, finding and cooking her own food, living alone in the family apartment. She loved every moment of it:

It was incredibly beautiful walking around Leningrad. It was completely empty. I was left all alone and it was the happiest time of my life. All of our books survived so I had an infinite number of books to read. I didn't go to school and I had quite a bit of money. We got money from my father's salary. I went around bookshops and the first book I bought was of the Dresden Picture Gallery. I also listened to records. It was absolute bliss.

School was starting up but, since there was no one to watch over her, she didn't bother to go. She passed the time doing whatever she wanted, spending her father's salary as she pleased. But all good things come to an end: 'Then, of course, an awful thing happened. My mother ... was allowed to go home.' This set off immense arguments as Vera tried to bring her daughter under some semblance of control, fights that did not end until she appealed to Nikolai to exert discipline from afar. 'She wanted total control over me. She was angry with me and wrote to my father complaining. His reply said, "My dearest, you may not have noticed but Larissa has grown up. You must show her some respect."'

Starting in September 1944, as there were no more excuses, she had to go to school, where she stayed for the next five years. Her experience was, not surprisingly, entirely different to that of

Francis. Even when some form of normal school life returned, it was a world away from that of an English education. She did not find school particularly stimulating, but she made good friends, several of whom she kept for life. One such was Natasha Davidova, who later became a biologist and was greatly liked by Francis. Another, younger friend was Olga Zabotkina, a ballet dancer whom Larissa – already a fanatical lover of ballet – admired and who later became an actress in the Soviet film industry. Although these three came from a highly privileged background by Soviet standards, this made little difference to the school they attended.

At about 14, it was usual for some of the children to join the Komsomol – the 'All-Union Leninist Young Communist League'

Larissa and Olga Zabotkina, *c.* 1953

– a Soviet equivalent of the Boy Scouts or the Hitler Youth. It organised worthy entertainment and tried to enforce high moral standards; according to Larissa, the first was tedious and the second was impossible. While it was most certainly a means of indoctrinating the young in the values of Communism, it also emphasised things like the strict equality of women, even if this was more a theoretical goal than a reality. It provided easily mobilised mass labour – members were required on occasion to participate in political programmes such as attacks on religion – and it was a feeder organisation identifying potentially valuable future members of the Party. Membership looked good on application forms for jobs or university places, and so many at her school tried to join even if they did so reluctantly. Larissa was initially rejected; applicants were vetted by older members, and she was considered too undisciplined, noisy and irreverent. She tried again a year or so later, because by that stage she was thinking of applying to the Academy of Fine Arts and was told by a teacher that having it on her application form could make all the difference:

Larissa, I must have a serious conversation with you. I know it does not matter to you very much, but when you apply to the Institute, it can affect whether they take you or not. There is no point in risking your entire future ... I know that this is your dream, and your life will suffer greatly if you are not accepted.

To make sure her application went through this time, she was told to become the mentor of a pupil at her school who was struggling to get through the end of year exams. So she did; the girl, an 8-year-old, was the daughter of a prostitute who was already being used for prostitution herself. Larissa took her home, got her mother to feed her, then spent a year reading to her and teaching her; all difficult tasks as the girl had never had a proper dinner sitting at a table, and knew little about how to talk to others. But Larissa persevered and 'at the end of the year, the girl safely moved to the second grade, and I was admitted to the Komsomol'. The connection was lost when Larissa left school soon after and she only saw her charge once more, walking down the street several years later: 'Someone flew at me, wrapped her arms around me, tightly, tightly, firmly held, held, and then let go.' The girl then walked away without a word: 'That was probably the best moment of my life. Apparently, for her, it was very important as well.'

# 4

# Francis: Paris, Army, Cambridge, 1946–1952

*First Experience of Paris – His Landlady and Her Daughter –*
*Russian Exiles – Uncle Max – Cinema, Food and*
*Collaborators – Homosexuality – National Service – Cambridge*

Francis was an indefatigable traveller in a period when few of his countrymen had ever travelled to European countries unless they were invading them. In the two decades between leaving school and getting married, he quit England as often as he could, going on multiple occasions to France, Italy, Spain, Portugal, Greece, Holland, Germany, Czechoslovakia, Poland, Yugoslavia, Belgium, Sweden and, after he met Larissa, to Russia. This need to leave the country was a central impulse, and one which consumed much of his very limited income. In the same period, the diaries record only two occasions when he travelled in his own country for pleasure, both short trips to visit friends in Newcastle and the Scottish Borders. In neither case did he see anything he considered to be worth noting.

If this habit set him apart from his countrymen, so did the way he was completely unaffected by the consumer revolution that swept across the country in the 1950s. While, at the government's urging, the English began to buy all manner of goods – cookers, fridges, televisions, radios and above all cars – all paid for after changes to the laws on consumer credit – he was largely immune to such temptations, never learning to drive and always living in accommodation which had lovely paintings, but little in the way of modern comfort.

The voyages abroad formed his character and gave him professional direction. It was while he was out of the country that he felt free from the constraints that English society imposed and which gave him what the historian Eric Hobsbawm later characterised as 'a face slightly melancholy in repose, with an air of hesitant diffidence'. I witnessed this myself; in England, he would sit, contorting his body in the chair, speaking quite jerkily in an often half-swallowed voice, rarely looking directly at the person he was addressing. He was the epitome of English self-repression, in fact. But in Italy or France, his entire manner changed, as did his voice – he waved his arms around with extravagance, spoke more loudly, with the delivery far more clear, direct and open. It is not surprising at all that his reputation was far higher in Europe than it was in Britain. In one he was a public figure, relaxed in the limelight. In the other he hid away, known to few and fully appreciated by fewer still.

This stark contrast showed up clearly in his diaries; while he was sociable, he preferred small gatherings, and was forever anxious about how well dinner parties had gone – had he performed, did people like him, did it all go well? Often enough he did not think it had. No such worries concerned him while he was travelling. Then he found he could make friends, and trust people far more easily; the constant fears about what people really thought of him faded. In 1964 the drama over Larissa made him ponder the contrast: 'I haven't really reflected enough how happy, even this year, I can be on those occasions with Enzo or Sandro at some pleasant restaurant ...' In Venice, he wrote that 'Friends here and in Rome have been as movingly wonderful as ever: and now I leave for Paris – and then a totally blank England ...' (10 July 1964). When he had returned to Cambridge from Italy in the spring he had noted that in Rome he had been 'quarreled over by two sets of friends and here there is NO-ONE ...' (26 April 1964).

His itinerant life began in the summer of 1946, immediately after leaving school, when he went on holiday with his family to France and was then left at 236 boulevard Raspail in Paris with an eccentric landlady, Mme Cécile Bondy, until he was called up in December. Here he had what might almost be called an epiphany; certainly, a suite of experiences which forever changed his course: sandwiched between a school dormitory and an army barracks, the contrast with life in Paris could not have been greater and no doubt created the romantic attachment he felt for the city. For the first time in his life, he was entirely free to do whatever he pleased. It is difficult to decide whether Paris was so wonderful because he could be himself, or whether it was because he could begin to find out who that was.

The city was not at its best. The war had caused relatively little physical damage, but a great deal of economic and psychological harm. There were shortages of nearly everything, and the atmosphere was soured by recrimination and suspicion. There were few cars yet on the roads due to petrol shortages, and bicycles everywhere. The occupying armies of the US and Britain still maintained a strong presence, and while Francis was there, the leaders of the Allied nations all arrived to negotiate the terms of a final peace treaty with the defeated countries, blocking many of the roads in the city centre while they did so. Domestic politics were fractious – many French people believed that either a Communist revolution or a Soviet attack was both inevitable and imminent, and the streets were regularly filled with demonstrations as politicians tried to devise a constitution which was both democratic and guaranteed to stop the very popular Communists from gaining power. As the final proposal was clearly going to be effective in achieving this latter goal, it triggered massive protests from the left, and counter-demonstrations from the right, when it was put to a referendum in October. Francis was caught up in one of these, although his status as an observer meant that he tended to play down the intensity and significance of the emotions involved:

> ... a thoroughly delightful evening; completed by my finding myself at 12 o'clock in the middle of a political demonstration at the place d'Opéra ... It was the night of the referendum, and as the results of the voting came in, they were broadcast by loudspeaker – 'Oui' or 'Non.' The chief demonstrators were a band of the 'Gaullist Union' who shouted 'De Gaulle au pouvoir' and 'Thorez au Poteau' ... There were two or three thousand people in all, shouting, singing the Marseillaise – the only unanimous action of the crowd – and chanting political slogans. I got the impression, however, that except for a small minority, people didn't really care about the result, and were only taking part for the sake of a 'rag' and were enjoying the whole thing immensely, as I was.[1] (14 October 1946)

The worlds of art and music, already a prime interest for him, were only slowly recovering, and many of the most famous figures were absent, unable to perform because they were accused of collaborating during the occupation – Serge Lifar, a choreographer, friend of Francis's father and another Russian exile – was banned from working until 1947. In Francis's view, all of the arts were hobbled both by an excessive reverence for the early

Modernists and by a facile attempt to interpret the previous five years of defeat and humiliation. All this he saw and catalogued, and loved the place the more for its sorry, bohemian state. Being there set the habits that lasted for the rest of his life: later on, Italy challenged and then supplanted France in his affections – he found it easier to develop close friendships with Italians – but Paris was his first love, as beautiful, exhilarating and alluring as only such loves can be.

His social circle was far wider than anything he had ever experienced before; in England his life had been school and his parents' friends and he only rarely met anyone from outside a very small section of the population. Paris was different, beginning with Mme Bondy, a somewhat disreputable art dealer who was herself under investigation for collaborating, although the case was dismissed while he was there.

> She combines the generosity of the German hausfrau (her husband had been a German Jew and she had spent the 1914–1918 war in Berlin) with the savoir-faire of the Frenchwoman. Her cooking is inimitable; she enjoys a vulgar joke and has a large store of them, which she tells one after the other, and then shakes with laughter and pokes me in the ribs ... [She] waddles around at an amazing speed and looks 45 ... she is not mean, but will get as much money out of anyone rich that she can: to the poor, she will lend readily. She is about the most sane 'practical woman' in the 'quartier' and consequently everyone comes to her for money and advice – she pretends to resent this furiously, but I think she rather enjoys it. She knows everybody in the art world, likes drink, and enjoys life out of which she certainly gets the best.[2]

She took him drinking around insalubrious bars, introduced him to prostitutes, black-marketeers and lesbians, told him dirty stories and gossip: 'last Tuesday I went to see "Vice" with Mme Bondy; there is quite a lot round here, all very carefully organised.' All of this he found fascinating, particularly the nearby Sphinx, the grandest brothel in Paris, with murals by Kees van Dongen. When it closed after the abolition of legal prostitution, he was there to witness the final moments:

> I went yesterday afternoon to the auction. The large hall was packed; chairs were stacked on the sides, people were sitting on the bar, and from the other end, flanked by the huge, ornate, ugly, naked, carved 'Sphinx' two fat oily auctioneers were roaring and selling sheets (ugh! What haven't those sheets concealed …?) when I asked a prostitute what she would do when the institution closed, she said 'I'll go to a factory,' and added, with perfect sincerity, 'But I don't think that it will be good for my health!' What answer could be better than that?! (13 October 1946)

He was also welcomed into the community of Russian exiles through his mother's family, met artists and composers and ballet dancers through his father, and spent a great deal of time on his own, simply wandering the streets, lost in a delirium of pleasure, alternating between the grand architectural sights and museums, and the insalubrious back streets of Montparnasse and Montmartre, which had not yet been taken over and turned into fake bohemian tourist spots. The period marks the first time his diary entries are not dominated by an undertone of depression, although anxiety about his forthcoming conscription frequently returned: 'Why can't I even write this diary with real joy? Why must there always be some misery to record …?' (10 October 1946).

Almost none of his new acquaintances had any money: most lived hand-to-mouth, in minuscule studio apartments, and were constantly borrowing off each other and coming up with unlikely schemes to make a fortune quickly. Most important was his main guide through the byways of the post-war city, the Virgil to his Dante, Baron Nicolas de Plater:

a Balt by birth but educated in Russia ... He spent his father's fortune in 13 years, living a reckless life largely in Paris, drinking, and, as far as I can make out, falling in love with boys and girls alike. He then went to paint in the flower shop in the rue de Seine of a very proletarian (to say the least) French woman, ugly, tasteless and mean, called Madeleine ... she will never be seen leaving the same house as him for fear of 'what the neighbours will say ...' The Baron is always borrowing money from Mme Bondy; once when she asked for some back, he replied witheringly 'Vous êtes bien française.' – this caused a row. In appearance the Baron is beautifully dressed in the shabbiest of clothes; He is rather small, but distinguished looking, always well shaved, with a trim, little moustache and his long, silvery hair carefully brushed back ... He gets drunk 'to forget his troubles for a while' – he is a fairly proud man, proud of his name ... and can never reconcile himself to the fact that he, Baron Nicolas de Plater, is ordered around by the scum of Paris. (1 November 1946)

The other important figure in this period was his maternal aunt's husband Mark Aldanov, Uncle Max. His books are now all but forgotten, but they were successful enough at the time for him to be nominated for the Nobel Prize thirteen times, although he never won it. His novels tended to be lengthy historical works

Mark Aldanov, *c.* 1955

rather in the manner of Tolstoy but, as he lived in exile and was violently anti-Bolshevik, they were not available in the Soviet Union and he had to earn what he could through articles, translations and sales to fellow exiles. Only his 1938 novel, *The Fifth Seal,* was successful enough to earn much money, although even this was hardly a page-turner. The *New York Times* commented:

> No more depressing spectacle could be conjured than the one Aldanov paints ... His characters for the most part are old men, broken, defeated, disillusioned, poor, hunted. The only two young people are a congenital syphilitic ... and a young Russian girl ... The plot moves with the speed of a glacier; the characters talk endlessly, doing little ...[3]

The Aldanovs decamped to America during the war to escape anti-Semitism, but their longing for Europe was so great that they all returned to France the moment it was possible to do so safely. They lived in a tiny apartment in the 8th arrondissement, while Francis's grandmother lived in Antibes, in accommodation so flea-ridden that few dared to visit her for more than a couple of hours. Francis itched for a week after disregarding the warnings.

Uncle Max was everything that his own father was not – expansive, uncritical and able to treat Francis seriously as an adult, perhaps the first person to do so. But he was heroically downbeat about life: 'oh! What a pessimist! "War with Russia, fifty-fifty – Bolsheviks will take Paris in a few days, but will be defeated by the atomic bomb. You will certainly get scarlet fever – etc etc"' (2 September 1946). He also met the Polonskis, who were the centre of the world of Russian exiles;[4] through them renewed his acquaintance with the dancer Nina Bibikova ('the nearest shaky equivalent to a girlfriend that I have': 5 August 1947); and was introduced to Russian high culture in exile:

On Tuesday at one o'clock I went to the Café Flore to meet Larionov as arranged; and we went to the little Categorie D restaurant 'Au Petit Saint Benois' (sic) where I met Goncharova.[5] We had a good lunch. After the general stinginess of the French, it was good to see the exaggerated largesse of the Russians. Larionov is like a huge bear, clumsy awkward and rather ugly, but extraordinarily good-natured, protective and friendly. He speaks French haltingly, whereas Goncharova is fluent. (I can't make out whether they are married or not – he introduces her as Goncharova, and she always refers to him as Larionov. They certainly live together). She is sweet, quietly dressed and respectable. Is this the designer of the flaming *coq d'or* décors?[6]

Larionov swept me into a taxi with him ('I'm always late; sometimes when Diaghileff asked me to call, I used to arrive on the wrong day') off to the Champs Elysées ... A piano was playing; there was a lot of excited Russian talking, kissing, shaking hands and cigarette offering all round. In the roomful of people there were a Russian dancer, Boris Knyaseff [sic], the Russian composer Tcherepnin, a host of handsome young men, a host of pretty young girls, one unidentified man.[7] The room was tiny, comfortable and a bit arty ... Tcherepnin ... played for me the music he has written for a new ballet, 'The butterfly and the something,'[8] which is really rather good, modern but with some good melody. It was all rather fun ... (1 October 1946)

A further discovery was food, which in Britain had never been good during Francis's lifetime – not only was restaurant culture still undeveloped (the first Italian restaurant in London only opened in the 1930s and, for most, eating out still meant either a hotel or a pub), rationing remained in place until the 1950s and was enforced fairly strictly. Institutional food, at school and later in the army, was little more than fuel designed to instil an indifference to the pleasures of life. In Paris, in contrast, the situation was similar to that which Larissa was experiencing in Russia – rationing in theory, but availability for all who could afford it:

Food, on the whole, is relatively plentiful, more so than in England, yet the rations remain ridiculously small – far too small to live on – and everyone resorts to the black market or the *Vente Libre*, where all foods can be found unrationed, but most expensive. Any system of control, such as exists in England, is totally disregarded ... With money in Paris today it is possible to live on a magnificent scale. For 1000 francs

(£2-2s) a superb meal with a good wine can be had, and is had in all the bigger restaurants in Paris ... a good meal can be had in a small restaurant without drink for 50frs (2/-); the 'category D' establishments offer a scanty menu for 32frs which, with the higher wages, appears to be within the limit of most.[9] (Essay on Paris, p. 4)

One thing Francis had was money – the relative states of the British and French economies meant that he could live well on what, in England, would have been very little. Getting hold of it was not so easy, however; exchange controls meant that English travellers were allowed only a limited amount of foreign currency, and so he had to borrow from family friends, who were then reimbursed when they travelled to England under similar constraints. But he had enough money to spend more time than most French people in restaurants, the variety of food and cuisine a daily reminder of his newfound freedom: 'excellent dinner, with wine, at Fouquet' (10 August 1946); 'lunch for 550frs with bouillabaisse and ½ a bottle of white wine' (1 September); 'a tremendous meal in the Café de la Paix (price 750 frs!!!) – ½ dozen oysters, kidneys, artichoke, peach melba, ½ bottle white Bordeaux, glass of cognac' (10 October); 'Dinner with Uncle Max, who is again in town; we ate at Prunier and had a marvellous meal: oysters, lobster, chicken, and dessert with an excellent wine' (24 October).

His other great entertainment, documented with even more care than his meals, was the cinema, which was his main contact with the rest of the world and later a connection with the similarly obsessed Larissa. Before the arrival of television – and it says much about Francis's background that Larissa's parents in Leningrad acquired a television before his did in London – the cinema was the prime entertainment across the classes. Both went at least once a week, and in Paris Francis went almost every day, sometimes twice a day. Until recently, Paris was an extraordinary place for seeing movies – there were hundreds of cinemas, ranging from the grandiose to the scruffy and tiny, showing a greater range of films from different countries than any other city on earth. But he was particularly enthralled by French productions, which he saw as further proof of French cultural superiority at all levels:

> On Thursday afternoon I went to see the highly praised French film 'Les enfants du paradis' … as good as anything I've yet seen in films … On Friday I saw for a second time the perfect French film 'La kermesse héroïque' – this is a real masterpiece. On Saturday afternoon I went to 'L'entraineuse' with Michèle Morgan …[10]

His difference to Larissa was that he vaguely disapproved of American movies, which were increasingly taking over the cinemas: '70 per cent of all films in Paris are American'.

> The Americans sometimes give a cold, cynical, intellectual, clever masterpiece – i.e. 'Double Indemnity' and 'Citizen Kane.' The good British film has the merits of sincerity and honesty, i.e., 'Brief Encounter' and 'The Way Ahead,' but are rather artificially acted and tend to lack subtlety. But who can produce films like 'La Femme du Boulanger,' 'César,' 'Carnet de Bal,' 'La Kermesse héroïque,' 'La grande illusion' – the list is endless.[11] (10 October 1946)

Francis was an acute observer, gifted at the rapid character sketch, but sometimes a rather naive one. This is illustrated most notably by his encounter with Rachel, his landlady's 34-year-old daughter, who lived with her mother and worked as a hairdresser. What he did not notice for years was that she would add to her income through casual prostitution. When she took him off to a seedy hotel in the nearby rue Sainte-Beuve, he was astonished by the assured way she went about it, surprised that the man at reception seemed to know her, and even more surprised that she tapped him for money for years afterwards. Eventually the penny dropped, and he came to like her a great deal, taking her out for dinner every time he visited Paris until the connection was lost in the late 1950s.

For the initial encounter, panic was inevitable. As Rachel coolly organised the room – 'Concierge: "Bien madame, ce sera pour une nuit?" Rachel (imperturbably): "Pas même – deux, trois heures seulement."' – he found all excitement and anticipation drain-

Francis and the Bondys, Paris, 1948

ing away: 'Never had women seemed less seductive ... I tried to imagine a thousand naked women dancing round me; I might as well have been in a London club for all the difference it made ... for a moment I thought of Eton and the headmaster's farewell talk ...' But it was too late to back out and all went reassuringly well: 'I flopped into my bed at two in the morning, exhausted but triumphant' (Essay on Rachel, pp. 14ff).

At that stage Rachel was concerned to keep her mother in ignorance, hence the hotel, but in the following years the Bondy family's finances deteriorated so much that Rachel began to conduct business at home and took up with a criminal belonging to a gang headed by 'Pierrot le Fou no. 2', a small-time crook called Pierre Carrot who managed to become the most celebrated criminal of the period by dint of being confused with someone else. Quite how Rachel became involved is not clear – Francis was too bashful to ask – but in 1949 he found himself going off to Fresnes Prison, taking the infamous felon cakes and clean laundry. His only regret was not getting to meet the man himself (2 September 1949).

Another entertainment was going to a purge trial – 'extraordinarily interesting and exciting, far more so than a play or film' (15 October 1946). These were the most prominent, and most controversial, events in the aftermath of the Liberation: more than 300,000 people were investigated on suspicion of having collaborated with the Nazis, and well over 100,000 were brought to trial. Those in the dock ranged from the leaders of the Collaborationist Vichy regime – the former president, Marshal Pétain, was condemned to death but had his sentence commuted – right the way down to women who slept with German soldiers, entertainers who performed for the occupying troops, and owners of shops and small businesses who sold goods to them. The trials were an attempt to impose proper legal procedure in order to stem the outburst of reprisals that attended the Liberation. No one knows how many were summarily executed by self-appointed committees and packs of roving vigilantes but government figures estimate more than 10,000 people were killed between 1944 and 1946.

The trial Francis attended was at the lower end of seriousness, concerning the activities of 'a factory owner called M. Maurice'. The whole tenor of the proceedings showed how the previously violent temperature was being tamed by the remorseless tedium of the law:

> The judge was courteous, polite and dignified, counsel was restrained and helpful. Maurice bore up well and answered forthrightly, but always quietly and the witnesses on the whole were brief and to the point. One is left with the impression that Maurice was guilty in the sense that he expected a German victory, and was determined to get the greatest possible benefits from such a victory, though quite likely he didn't actively desire it; was not anti-Semitic, but was prepared to profit from any difficulties in which Jews found themselves, was personally brave and helped friends and those in difficulties; was generally fairly indifferent to the fate of his country.

> Francis found it all very thought-provoking: he had expected to hear evidence of evil, but found mere ordinariness, a tale of simple people doing their best to survive in extraordinary circumstances and with no energy left over to worry about matters of principle.

> In this way the trial was a trial against France – millions must have behaved like him; people who were not wicked, but who were opportunists; people who were not thieves, but

who were not too honest either. One would like to put on trial judge, jury, witnesses, counsel and audience and know what exactly their part was under the occupation.

He also realised that it was mere good fortune that he, as an Englishman, was able to watch with such distance and objectivity:

> looking among some pornography on a 'Rive Gauche bouquin' I came across the Marquess of Londonderry's (who now plays bridge with mummy) Penguin book on Germany, where the unfailing 'courtesy and charm of Goering, Ribbentrop and Neurath,' and so on come in for a lot of praise.[12] And where are Goering and Ribbentrop? Awaiting tomorrow's hanging in Nuremberg. And Lord Londonderry? I rather suspect in our expensive house in London ... (15 October 1946)

---

For all that Francis described his encounter with Rachel in a jocular manner, it was an important moment for him because of his overwhelming fear that he was homosexual, a worry that had gripped him since before he began writing his diary and which continued to assail him for years afterwards. It is impossible to give an account of him and Larissa without dealing with this subject, not least because many of Francis's colleagues assumed that theirs was a *mariage blanc*, an arrangement merely of mutual advantage and no more. Larissa married Francis because she wished to escape to the West; Francis married Larissa to cover up his homosexuality. Neither was true. Certainly, Larissa had no burning desire to come to the West, and hated the assumption that she was in some way a defector. She was a member of the

Soviet elite, well placed in one of the greatest museums in the world, living in a milieu which she found endlessly stimulating. Falling in love with an Englishman and leaving her home for a rainy little island with bad food and indifferent plumbing was the last thing she needed.

Nor did Francis fit into any of the categories we know today – not repressed, not in the closet. Rather, his life was a constant struggle, played out in the pages of his diaries, to escape the cold-ness of the world he was raised in, and this was reflected in his understanding of his sexuality. He was sent away as a boarder to a preparatory school at the age of 8, and never again returned home to his parents except for holidays. His father was often enough an absentee, his mother intrusive and directing. They allowed their children little freedom to form their own views, while simultane-ously rejecting any real responsibility for their upbringing.

School was worse, until he began to find a small group of boys with whom he had something in common in his last year. One was George Cary, a gifted linguist with a passion for Persian poetry. Cary was, like Francis, an atypical Etonian, the son of Joyce Cary, an Anglo-Irish novelist whose income was so erratic his family was occasionally plunged into homelessness and poverty.[13] Cary was one of the very few with whom Francis could discuss books, music, art without the fear of ridicule. Even so, such friendships retained a distance: the moment that another friend, called Walter Poole, allowed first name terms was an important milestone – 'the goodbyes were heartrending – especially the one with Walter – he has now invited me to call him this ...' (8 August 1946). Cary waited until long after he had left school before permitting such familiarity.

The relationships that did develop in such circumstances were extraordinarily intense. This was inevitable; deprived of any other form of emotional support at the height of adolescence, a little group of exclusively male friends of necessity formed the entire universe. They learned how to converse, interact, feel affection and express emotion primarily through each other, and this naturally tended to reinforce attitudes and behaviour. The results were often strange, the emotions extravagant and the consequences long-lasting. When fellow art historians Anthony Blunt and Ellis Waterhouse – both somewhat older – were at the British School at Rome in the 1930s, they talked always in the schoolboy patois of Marlborough, which both emphasised their closeness and served to make others feel like outsiders. The German-Jewish art historian Ernst Gombrich – entirely immune to the power of such social messaging – was one of the few with the distance and self-confidence to find this more infantile than elitist.[14]

The behaviour resulted in a total detachment from the society in which they lived, and a misogyny so profound that few truly overcame it, or even wanted to. The disdain blended with an exaltation of male company with strong homoerotic overtones, a combination of half-digested Greek philosophy and profound ignorance. At one stage at Eton, Francis and his cohort were given a lecture on the sin of Onanism, an offence against God and Nature, condemned as dangerous by Church and Medicine alike. The problem was that the teacher could not bring himself to explain what it was, so they left the room more confused than ever. When homosexual acts were discovered, condemnation was swift: Francis's friend, the novelist Simon Raven, was expelled from Charterhouse, and notes in Francis's diaries expressed a repugnance at the very idea of physical contact. In a notebook many years later, he wrote that he could remember no such events from his time at school at all and that 'the Cambridge I knew when I came up, but now completely vanished, of ageing virginal homosexuality' did not permit real relationships: 'A "real relationship" ... would have involved a prison sentence ...'[15]

But the heightened emotions remained and had to be fitted into a rationale which valorised the feelings while keeping a distance from the dangers of the practice. George Cary, for example, was desperately obsessed with a younger boy called Tony Lloyd – who was evidently entirely ignorant of his importance – and wrote long letters to Francis to describe his misery.[16] So far, so conventional; it was the rationalisation which is interesting. His infatuation was because he resembled a girl: 'I have seen a girl ... she has the Tonian eyes and Tonian hair, and makes me feel very sad whenever I see her' (Cary to FH, 2 September 1945). And he was careful to parse his longing with great care: he drew a careful distinction between love and lust, between Plato and Freud: 'As for Freud's explanation of the outward phenomena of homosexuality, it is ingenious and filthy; but these outward phenomena do not apply, I am sure, to myself' (Cary to FH, 4 October 1945). His passion was of the Platonic sort, filtered through *fin-de-siècle* aestheticism: a love of pure beauty, and of intellectual beauty: boys as an abstract conception, not as creatures of flesh and blood. There was space, therefore, for some sort of lower attraction to girls. After one particularly long and extravagant account of the beauty of his chosen ideal, he added: 'I am really almost in love with the Rosemary girl ...' (Cary to FH, 12 December 1945).

This was an approach which Francis also adopted, and to a certain extent his anguish stemmed largely from the binary categories which had emerged from nineteenth-century medicine, which created an ever starker division between hetero- and homosexuality and allowed for nothing in between. Francis, like many of his class and generation, found great solace in the company of other men, and in the close friendships with them. His ideal evening was sitting in a pub or in his room at King's, with a glass of whisky and the company of a couple of male friends he had known for years, with whom there were no emotional complications and who made him feel comfortable and safe. Such people had fulfilled many of the roles normally allotted to parents ever since he was dispatched to school. Couples occasionally did the same, and he loved 'being invited out by couples who, I suppose, act as substitute families for me' (27 October 1963).

But increasingly he found it difficult to separate these sorts of friendships from ideas of sexuality. This he ultimately came to blame on 'the effects of Freudianism. I maintained that this had put personal relations on a very different basis. Romantic friendships (eg Hallam and Tennyson) were now looked on as something shameful ...'(11 January 1951).[17] He rejected absolutely what he considered such a coarsening of human relationships; as far as he was concerned, the value of these male friendships was precisely because they had no physical component.

Cary divided relationships into three categories, these characterised in turn by love, lust and friendship. Francis's great search – and the quality that made him different to many of his peers – was the ill-defined need to bring all three together into one person. 'On the surface I can continue for weeks, months living happily with the many friends I have here, and then suddenly, deep down, something cracks, and I desperately need a real friendship, something much more emotional than the more superficial ones I am used to ...' (9 June 1950).

As the memory of school became dimmer, so the intellectual justifications lost their appeal, and the passions faded also. Within a few months Cary was writing that 'the memory of Tony is beginning to slip a little, slip a few cogs, and once I have started to forget, the end has begun' (Cary to FH, 15 May 1946). So it had: the following year he announced: 'You may have heard of my adventures with Mig; I proposed to her at the ball, and ... she accepted.'[18]

The anguish, the swooning, the epic poetry written for the beloved were gone; in their place was a practical arrangement which, nonetheless, worked well enough until Cary's premature death in 1953. There is no hint of grand passion: writing of his fiancée he said, 'such is woman, *mutabile semper*. Their brains are all wool, they don't think out anything logically'; and his expectations of marriage were decidedly limited: 'I am sure I shall never be happy until I can find someone stupid enough to marry me …' (Cary to FH, 15 May 1946). Later he announced a visit to Cambridge 'with Margaret there for a bit to look after me, to comb my hair and wash it …' (Cary to FH, 12 November 1949). It was a fragmented love: practical, maternal, companionable, with little space either for passion or intellectual partnership. The friendship and closeness derived from a shared background and education remained an exclusively masculine concept.

Just as Cary explained himself by reference to Plato, Pico della Mirandola and Marsilio Ficino, Francis in his diaries constantly referred back to literature to describe scenes, people or moments, to the point that life and literature often seem to blend together, with each explaining the other: '[Venturi] reminds me of a Norman Douglas character …' (10 July 1954); 'Brindisi is … utterly Graham Greene territory' (13 July 1954); 'Mlle de G[asparin], tall and angular – straight out of Corneille …' (3 September 1954); 'He reminds me of the gardener in the Edith Sitwell poem' (12 July 1952). Such references turned up in letters and in conversation as well, as a form of shorthand to communicate ideas, and a way of signalling who you were to others. They were, of course, rather meaningless to most people. It was a form of communication never entirely direct in expression, self-consciously stylised – and was not at all possible with someone like a poorly educated girl from a Wiltshire estate like Cary's new wife.

Cary did not think it possible or necessary to bring the pieces together, and he may have been correct not to try. Certainly, the difficulties of attempting to do so afflicted Francis for many years. He emerged from Eton half convinced that his desperation for emotional intimacy meant that he was homosexual, despite fervent reading at the time of reassuring educational textbooks saying that such feelings were perfectly usual in adolescent boys. In this area, his own family background was unhelpful. Cary came from a family which had sent its children to public schools for generations and was perfectly used to such emotions; at one stage he recounted a conversation with his mother about his unrequited love, with his mother giving advice and recommending another boy as being prettier. Francis's family, on the other hand, had far more conventional views: his mother badgered him about girlfriends, his father lectured him on condoms and his beloved Uncle Max gave instructions on prostitutes. Everything else met their disapproval:

> Heated family discussion at dinner about homosexuality –
> how far it should be tolerated, etc. I violently disagreed with
> just about everything that was said … Not that homosexual-
> ity is a good thing – in fact, I believe very much the reverse,
> but that absolute toleration is not only completely essential,
> but so obvious as not even worth discussing … yet daddy
> suggests there is too much … (22 December 1950)

And so he anguished for years, debating whether to go to a prostitute in 1946: 'What are the pros and cons – Pro: If I am, as I am, homosexually inclined and if I really enjoyed sexual experience with a woman, it might change everything and remove my most serious worry' (1 September 1946). Every little event reassured or threw him into despair: 'Oh God, if I'm homosexual

I shall kill myself ...' (28 January 1946). Then hope re-emerged: 'Saturday night was possibly the first time that I've really kissed a girl properly and I enjoyed it very much indeed – now that's worth thinking about!'(15 September 1947). But perhaps, as a beginner, he was aiming a little too high. That first kiss was with a 22-year-old called Zizi Jeanmaire, a ballet dancer who was on the brink of becoming one of the first major celebrities of the tele-vision age in France, the muse to Yves Saint-Laurent, in almost the same league as Brigitte Bardot.[19] Her 1949 performance in *Carmen* prompted the *Guardian* to write in her obituary that 'Nothing as sensual ... had been seen on the London stage before'. Francis was entranced from the moment he met her: 'Zizi ... of an indefinable beauty, is, possibly, in a bright summer frock and her curls coming over her face, the most lovely thing I have ever

Zizi Jeanmaire in Monaco, 1946

87

seen. With her laughing smile, she is Spring in Paris, Champagne, all the pleasant clichés in the world' (4 September 1947). She was perfectly friendly, gave him a photo of herself and a hand-painted paper plate, but did not return the admiration.

The mores of the age meant that not being homosexual produced almost as much anguish as being so: none could escape easily. Like Cary, and even many of those who were less confused, Francis could not relate to girls at any level as equals. Indeed, the only times he comes across in the diaries as unpleasant are when they come into view: even Rachel Bondy he initially described as 'an intelligent, too intelligent, bitch with impeccable taste and serious, too serious, views on life' (10 October 1946). Others were similarly dismissed: 'Ruth is a nice girl, but I wish she'd shave' (16 March 1950). 'Peggy Cripps to tea – a fat girl of quite

Painted plate, inscribed 'A mon cher Francis, en souvenir de cette
memorable soirée ... London 6 août 1947'

phenomenal plainness ... like a Ronald Searle cartoon ...' (22 March 1950).[20] Curiously, this savage misogyny generally came into play only in England and largely stopped after he graduated from Cambridge. When he separated from the closed worlds of school and King's, and was no longer so desperate to blend in by adopting their values and style, such malevolence ceased. But girls from his own country he always found quite impossible: 'how can one love those pedestrian, dull, English girls?' (10 September 1947). Intelligent women he found unfeminine, feminine ones he found unintelligent, and he didn't know what to do with either. On the rare occasion he encountered both qualities in the same person – for example, when he met the future journalist and author Katherine Whitehorn at a meeting organised by 'six Newnham girls, who wish to show that intellect and feminine charm can be combined' – he had no idea what to think except 'She is pretty and smart' (31 January 1950).

He adored the young dancer Nina Bibikova, whom he met in 1946 when she came with the Roland Petit ballet to London, but found that they really had nothing to talk about, and had the same problem with every other girl he encountered. One was a young painter called Dora Holzhandler (1928–2015). She was gentle, attractive, talented, Jewish, brought up in France, and intelligent. She was lovely, except that she was dreamily mystical and profoundly un-intellectual – an 'archetypal hippy' as her obituary in 2015 put it. The relationship only lasted a few months, with Francis convincing himself that she loved him more than he loved her, and self-indulgently concerned about hurting her. That was an error: when she unceremoniously dumped him in a letter – 'This is to say good bye ... you do not love me ...' (14 March 1950) – he was more wounded than relieved. Even worse, she went off and married someone else so quickly that he was offended as well.

Dora Holzhandler and Francis, by Dora Holzhandler, *c.* 1950

There is little to be said about Francis's time in the army, beyond the fact that he loathed every moment of it – 'Resolution for New Year: Kill myself' (1 January 1947) – and emerged with one good, if troubled, friend in a painter called John Eyles, who was a constant presence in his life for nineteen years until he took a dislike to Larissa. Francis's reaction to the army was not exceptional; very few enjoyed their period of conscription, not least because they saw quite clearly that the entire exercise was utterly pointless and unfair – after the First World War conscription ended swiftly, after the Second it continued for another fifteen years. The whole programme left behind little of worth, beyond a prodigious number of novels, plays and poems complaining about how horrible and ridiculous it all was, a deeply ingrained dislike of militarism in those who went through it, and the occasional call for its reintroduction from those concerned about the imminent collapse of British civilisation through moral decadence and the corroding effects of rock and roll.

Francis was very much in the pacifist camp, although unwilling to become a conscientious objector; he noted that he didn't object to war in principle, he merely disliked the idea of being involved in it personally – a view which he readily acknowledged was as morally unsound as it was strong. This persuaded him not to try to evade conscription, even though he could have done so, as he had in his possession a letter testifying that he was subject to homicidal and suicidal impulses, and presented a clear danger to himself and others unless he received immediate treatment: 'When I went to London last weekend, I met the psychologist mother of Haino [Maas, a school friend] who has written for me a letter ... certifying that ... I'm a lunatic ...' (17 December 1946). He kept the letter as a keepsake and as an emergency parachute if he found military life unbearable.

Even when it became clear that he would not be sent anywhere dangerous, his dislike persisted, although the limited diary entries suggest his time was far from being completely intolerable. There was the discomfort, the cold and the poor food, but there was an annual holiday, which he used to go to France, and he had regular leaves, which permitted plenty of time at the opera and theatre and in restaurants in London. His most miserable period was during basic training in Yorkshire, in the middle of the coldest winter Britain had endured for a very long time, which resulted in coal shortages, interrupted food supplies and power cuts.

Curiously, the weather was not something that featured overmuch in the diaries. Glorious days in Italy, disappointing downpours in Sicily are frequently mentioned, as are long lunches in the sun in Greece, but only because of the emotions aroused or because of the effect on the landscape. Being cold in England was a normal condition, and it would seem that Francis, and most of his fellow countrymen, accepted the much lower temperatures then as unexceptional and not worth comment, even though few homes – and certainly not schools or Cambridge colleges – had central heating. Far more important than the discomfort, and a topic to which he returned again and again, was the absurdity of military life; he spent much time dreaming of all the better things he could have been doing to fill up his time. His response was to try and forget it ever happened: 'If I ever write an autobiography, these two years will remain blank pages'(4 February 1947).

Eventually he was transferred to the Royal Electrical and Mechanical Engineering Corps and a camp near Bicester in Oxfordshire, where he was promoted to sergeant and given the task of trying to teach the many recruits who were functionally illiterate to read and write. This he found better, but still dispiriting: 'the work consists largely of organisation but includes a lot of instruction for sub- sub-literates to quite bright people. The standard of education ... is unbelievably low ... I am subject to a good deal of unpopularity. Education is universally despised and disliked' (4 September 1947). Even worse, he discovered he was less than enthused by teaching – worrying, as one of the professions he was already considering would involve a good deal of it:

In front of me are rows of men sitting in a dingy, ill-lit Nissen hut writing an essay on whether the Death Penalty should be abolished – as if they care! ... How lucky they don't realise that my will over them is so weak that at any moment it may give way & then what? There are few things more unpleasant than going into a class and not knowing what you are going to say ... You almost pray for them to help you, but they merely look stolid and silent and furtively hide the *Daily Mirror* under the desk. (5 December 1947)

Although it all came to an end in 1949, his time served and normality restored, the after-effects lingered – not because of any psychological trauma, but because all who passed through the system remained as reservists, liable to be called up in case of a further war. This was not a merely theoretical possibility. The Soviet blockade of Berlin in 1948 and the subsequent Western airlift to sustain it could easily have spilled over into open conflict; the business of dismantling the British Empire caused a periodic demand for troops in places like Malaya and the Middle East; and the outbreak of the Korean War in June 1950 sent panic through the many ex-servicemen who had assumed that their reservist status was a formality. Francis's category was never chosen for anything, but it was a constant fear in the background for several years. 'In the mornings with the paper, I almost shake with terror … I am really far more frightened of the preliminaries than of death itself. It's the cold, the carrying of equipment, the barracks, the sergeant-majors, which terrify me …' (30 November 1950).

---

His patriotic duty done, in October 1949 Francis moved from barracks to university, starting his course at King's College Cambridge. He had some acquaintances there already, as King's, once known as 'Eton in the Fens', still took a large portion of its students from Francis's school. Both were founded by Henry VI in the fifteenth century, and King's only began to accept non-Etonians because of enforced reforms in the mid-nineteenth century. But if it retained a close association, it was stripped of all the elements that had made school life so unpleasant. For a start,

Francis changed subject: quite why he ever thought becoming a doctor was a good idea is unclear, although the possibility of being excused National Service if he was studying medicine played a part. He had taken the entrance examinations in physics and chemistry, was accepted, and then decided that spending the rest of his life dealing with ill people was far too high a price to pay even to get out of the army.

So he switched to history and began the first period in his life when he felt at ease in his surroundings. It was like living in a reverse image of his previous experience: everything that made him marginal at school was now valued. 'I never dreamt when I went to school that I would look forward to the beginning of term, and be sorry at the end of term. Yet such is the magic of Cambridge' (18 March 1950). Being intellectual was more esteemed than being sporty; being described by the politics fellow Noel Annan as 'a hopeless intellectual' (10 January 1950) was now a compliment that made him glow with pleasure, not a prelude to being bullied and humiliated. Friends were easier to make and more stimulating: 'every day almost I have long and interesting conversations' (31 January 1950). But the place nagged at him nonetheless: he instinctively rebelled against the very nature of the English and saw himself as apart from them, 'good looking and charming and dull' as they were in his eyes. He found it hard to adjust to the frequent cruelty masquerading as wit or unconventionality which was so valued. The tendency of one friend to be deliberately contrary in argument and never take anything seriously made him 'the perfect example of the upper middle class Englishman with his virtues and vices equally marked' (2 January 1950).

For all that, Francis became deeply attached. Infused by the relaxed mores of Bloomsbury because of the presence and influence of people like John Maynard Keynes and E. M. Forster, King's was far more open and egalitarian than other colleges, and encouraged much more mixing between fellows and students than was the norm.[22] It had an unusually liberal approach to life – having girlfriends in rooms overnight; ostentatiously bringing a boyfriend to a party or to High Table, as E. M. Forster did – encouraging an atmosphere of tolerance and openness that was remarkable for the time, and radically different to any other college in Cambridge or in the country more generally. This he valued, referring frequently to 'the wonderful liberty we have at Kings' (18 November 1950) and 'the King's ethos' (9 February 1951).

But openness was dependent on exclusivity: a members-only form of liberalism and tolerance which did not extend too far beyond the college gates and served to make the students still more isolated from the rest of the country. Homosexuality was accepted in a way that did not become common in Britain for another half century – but gay men knew that however much they could be themselves inside this world, just outside lay the possibility of prison or chemical castration, as was the case with the mathematician and code breaker Alan Turing, also of King's, who was convicted of gross indecency in March 1952. Moreover, women were interlopers and on the whole remained consumer goods if they were not actively despised; students who were not from the great public schools scarcely figured at all.

Francis was glad to be included in the college's warm embrace, but was always afflicted by a sense of fraud, a feeling that he would be somehow found out and rejected. He was constantly at social gatherings, but never at home in them: 'For me, the triumph of the evening was that I wasn't, as always, outside myself, observing' (19 February 1950). He always had this nagging sense that he didn't truly belong: 'After a few hours of the high life, I returned to the world I really belong to ... I always feel like a poor relation' (12 May 1950). Moreover, these insecurities blended with his ever-present fear of being attacked:

I enjoyed listening to the music: as, indeed, I would have done this time, if I hadn't had to pretend to be something that I can never be – brilliant, amusing, sociable etc. If only I could have been left to myself! As it was, I tried to turn myself into the buffoon – the Jew in Dostoevsky's 'House of the Dead' that character who has haunted my imagination ever since I read that wonderful book. (21 February 1952)

Nonetheless, he responded to the place, doing exceptionally well in the first set of exams in 1950 – 'success is wonderfully pleasant' (17 June) – then changing to English for the last year. When he graduated, King's offered funding to write a thesis that might lead to a college teaching fellowship – doctorates were vulgarities suitable only for Germans or Americans – but on condition that he went away. So, in early 1952, he left for Italy, and did not come back for two years.

# 5

# Larissa: School, Academy, Hermitage, 1944–1962

*Rules and How to Break Them – A Run-Down Dacha –*
*Forgery – Entrance to the Academy – Stalin – The Doctors'*
*Plot – Dobroklonsky – Stealing a Corpse – Potatoes and*
*Tourniquets – Cirrhosis and the KGB – Joining the Party –*
*Finding a Husband – Losing a Husband*

One of Larissa's defining characteristics was her indifference to rules, although she was far from being the only Russian with this outlook. Her love of country co-existed quite easily with total disdain for its rulers. Just as she spent little time reading the newspapers or listening to the news on the radio, so equally she did her best to ignore the rules and procedures that the government introduced and changed with regularity. She honed her skills at school, forging signatures on school reports. Others behaved in the same way: the local street market where her mother bought fresh eggs and milk and vegetables was completely illegal, but many of the local police also bought food there, so it continued unmolested. While food bought officially was in short supply and of poor quality, the produce supplied unofficially was abundant and fresh – when she came to England, she was appalled by the tastelessness of the chickens, the age of the eggs and – above all – the lack of cheap, high-quality caviar.

So, while Francis was meticulous about following the rules – the consequence of punishments meted out for the least infringement of school regulations from the age of 8 – Larissa had a more impressionistic approach. Sensing what you could get away with, knowing how to negotiate the system in a society which could not have functioned had everyone been law-abiding, was a great but necessary skill: 'you could only exist if you constantly broke the law. Nobody abroad ever quite understood this.' Loyalty to

Larissa in 1952

country was expressed through loyalty to family, friends and, in Larissa's case, the institution which ultimately housed her, the Hermitage. The government was distant, and no one expected much of leaders.

This attitude was deeply ingrained and was learned primarily from her family. Her uncle – arrested, imprisoned and tortured for no reason whatsoever – demonstrated the simple fact that honesty and a sense of duty gave no protection. The state could still strike like lightning and hit anyone at any time. As you could be punished even if you had done nothing wrong, then the incentive to be honest shrank away. Larissa's father was himself

Robert Spiegler

an expert at weaving a path through the thickets of government and bureaucracy in order to protect his family and friends. After the Caucasus and Crimean campaigns, he had been transferred to the Soviet Eastern Front in preparation for war against Japan. 'But, literally, the moment they made peace with Japan, Dad asked for retirement and came back.' He had not been home to Leningrad for nearly five years and, after nearly thirty years in the military, he could take no more. He retired, even though it meant a reduced pension, then found a job working as head of security in a Leningrad armaments factory. 'He had a very nice secretary but there was nothing to do.' He returned a changed man; the experience of the war and the purges had made him introverted, gloomy and almost reclusive. His mood was additionally deepened when he learned that Vera had been having an affair with a Jewish engineer called Robert Spiegler ('during the war he had constant trouble because he was always being arrested as a German spy').

My mother had quite a long affair with him. She managed to keep it very quiet so nobody knew. But she told her closest friends and one of them decided she would marry my father when he returned from the war. So she invited my father over when my mother was on holiday and told him.

Nikolai exploded with disappointment and rage, confronted his wife and threatened to shoot them all, including Larissa, if she left. Vera was terrified, and broke it off immediately, perhaps assisted in her decision by the now 14-year-old Larissa, who seemed quite relaxed about the threat of being shot and came down on her father's side: 'I said that, if she left, I would stay with him.' This was not because of any shock or even disapproval at her mother's behaviour, though; she was very fond of Spiegler, whom she had known for years. 'I knew everything that was happening

[and] liked him very much. He was so fond of me. Even after my mother stopped seeing him, he would phone me and invite me to restaurants.' When Spiegler died a few years later, Larissa went alone to the funeral at the Jewish cemetery.

The problem was that Nikolai and Vera loved each other deeply, but in different ways. Although he had a fairly basic approach on occasion – 'He said throughout his life that any woman can be bought' – nonetheless he was 'completely the sort of person who just loved one woman for life'. Vera was devoted as well, so much so that she had a nervous breakdown when he died in 1961. But it was not born out of passionate attraction, although it did develop into a deep affectionate attachment – love, certainly, but of a different sort.

After this traumatic return, Nikolai became ever more reclusive, keeping up contact with only a few old acquaintances, not least because he began to weaken from the onset of the heart disease that ultimately killed him. One such friend was Vladislav Tregubov, the colleague who had protected Vera and Larissa during the siege and who was targeted in the early stages of Stalin's attack on the leaders of Leningrad in the late 1940s, taking violent revenge for the threat that their courage and success during the siege posed for his position. Tregubov was a close friend and Larissa adored him. Like so many others, his personal life was chaotic: 'He began an affair with one of the young soldiers in his regiment. She had a child but ... after the war, his wife returned and found out ... She made a terrible fuss and we all hated her ...' He had always been vulnerable – he was not only, like Nikolai, from a noble family, his father Rostislav had been a prominent anti-Bolshevik, monarchist and secretary of the anti-Semitic and ultra-national-ist Union of the Russian People before he vanished in 1917.[1] His son, like Nikolai, continued to serve the new regime in the army, but if Nikolai found his progress slowed because of his family,

Tregubov was in a much worse position, and when the Leningrad purge began he was arrested and charged with misappropriating army funds to build himself a luxurious dacha in the country-side. He was accused of using draftees as labourers, stealing army equipment to install electricity and run power lines illegally from a nearby substation. This was serious; if found guilty, he would have been stripped of his rank and at the very least sent to the Gulag.

Nikolai was outraged at the cynicism and manifest injustice of the charges, drove out and photographed the dacha, then went to Moscow and spent months going to army hearings and Party disciplinary meetings, using the photographs to demonstrate that the so-called luxurious dacha was, in fact, little more than a run-down hut scarcely capable of standing upright. Nobody could possibly think any money at all had been spent on it for years, and his evidence clearly proved that Tregubov was innocent, and the claims trumped-up nonsense by vindictive enemies jealous of his competence and rank.

Astonishingly, the officials were eventually convinced, both by the photographic evidence and by Nikolai's persistence and righteous indignation. Unlike many in this period, Tregubov was cleared and returned to active service. The debt of friendship incurred during the siege was paid.

But, as Larissa observed, 'It was just as well they didn't see any pictures of the inside. It was like a palace. Filled with treasures.'

I asked whether that meant he really had been misappropriating funds.

The question puzzled her. 'Of course.'

Vera also knew how to short-circuit the system and get away with it. When the siege began, she started to work in an office that was issuing ration books, but the process was far too slow considering the urgency. The forms had to be filled in, deposited, carefully checked and authorised, and then countersigned by the office manager, who was himself overburdened by work. 'Usually, you had to wait at least a week ... so she signed all the documents herself. She gave them back so people could get the ration cards straight away. She was like me – foolish, but brave in her foolishness.'

Larissa's own efforts in this direction began when she was fairly young, forging her mother's signature on the school reports she never bothered to hand over, and writing letters to her teacher in her mother's handwriting so she could have days off. Later she graduated to ration cards, when she mastered the art of faking official stamps by cutting a raw potato into the shape required and pressing it into an ink pad. Once perfected, this technique could be used for other purposes as well, and she remained enormously proud of the occasion when her mother wished to take a group of friends to the opera and Larissa forged all the tickets so that they could sit in the best seats. 'They were terribly upset when they found out afterwards.'

Judgement was all, and having a convincing tale ready to go was crucial: when confronted in 1953 with some exams in philosophy for which she had done no work and in which she had no great interest, she told the examiner as she stood up to answer questions that she could not speak because of Stalin's death a few days previously. 'I was not very well versed in dialectical materialism, and so when it was my turn I said, "You know, I'm so upset that I can't answer!" The examiner replied, "I understand, I understand," and passed me anyway.'

She began the five-year course at the Leningrad Academy of Fine Arts in 1949 – starting about the same time as Francis began his own degree at Cambridge. The Academy, also known as the Repin Institute, had been the national institute for arts training until that was moved to Moscow in 1947, but it remained highly prestigious and getting in involved passing a competitive exam in addition to meeting the normal requirements for higher education. Although primarily an academy to train artists, it had a small faculty of art history, and this is what Larissa applied to join. Her success meant that she avoided the much more basic courses at the University of Leningrad and began what she described as one of the most exciting periods of her life: 'I can't begin to describe how wonderful it was. To begin with, there were only twelve people in each year. In comparison, the university … took one hundred and twenty students a year. You can imagine the extraordinary attention we were given.'

It was, in other words, an elite group, fast-tracked for rapid promotion and with access to many of the most knowledgeable and influential people in the art world, some of whom were their teachers. The group she was in bonded swiftly, with some remaining lifelong friends. 'When we first met, we liked each

The Academy of Fine Arts, St Petersburg

other so much that we didn't want to go home.' The courses were intensive and thorough, so that she emerged with a far superior formal training than Francis could ever have found in England. The social range was also far wider than he experienced, from people more or less drawn from the same section of Soviet society as Larissa herself, through to a girl, Olga Lesnizkaya, who came from a desperately poor family: 'Before coming to lectures at nine o'clock, she would go to the Hermitage to work as a cleaner to earn money for food.' Like Larissa, Olga won a permanent job at the Hermitage; she joined the Classical sculpture department, and stayed there for the rest of her career.

The education was based on the Germanic model introduced before the Revolution and which continued because so many of the teachers, and curators in the museum system, had managed to hang on to their posts. Many were, once more, from the old nobility, but were reluctantly accepted by the new regime for the same reason that Larissa's father and uncle were allowed to continue their careers in the military. For all its dislike of class and privilege, the Soviet regime mixed an unpredictable understanding of the importance of expertise with the periodic violence of purges and persecution. It also valued high culture, to the extent that rather than wanting to obliterate it as a symbol of class, it was to be celebrated, and art, music, ballet and literature made available to everyone, even if they sometimes had to be reconfigured and reinterpreted to fit in with Communist doctrine. This made the Soviet Union into something of a paradise for people with tastes like Larissa, who fell in love with ballet at the age of 5, spent many of her schooldays going to poetry readings at the Palace of Pioneers, and then began to form her interest in the visual arts after the siege.

There were courses on political economy, dialectical materialism, Soviet and European history, ancient, medieval and modern art, criticism, teaching, curatorship, and conservatorial methods. Alongside the more formal lectures, there were lessons in painting and drawing, as it was thought that practical knowledge was essential for a proper understanding of art. Larissa emerged as a competent draughtswoman, able to earn extra money to supplement her income by illustrating books. The ancient world was taught by the curator of antiquities at the nearby Hermitage, with accompanying lectures from the museum's director. Medieval art lectures were delivered by an architect who had spent much of his youth in Turkey and had developed an obsession with the Hagia Sophia. So they studied that for the entire year rather than getting the overview the course specified: 'We all adored it [but] when it came to the exams we knew nothing about French medieval architecture because we had only learnt about the Middle East.' The third year was seventeenth-century Baroque – the subject that Francis was slowly approaching in a very different fashion – then the Renaissance, the eighteenth century, and Russian art. But no Impressionism or Modernism, as those were still considered to be decadent and unacceptable, even though the Hermitage had one of the finest collections of both in the world.

The course seemed almost designed for Larissa, so much so that she graduated at the head of her year, rated as excellent in all assessed courses – even the mandatory ones in Marxism–Leninism and the dialectical materialism that she professed to know nothing about – and so was awarded one of the coveted permissions to go straight on to a three-year post-graduate study programme at the Hermitage. Others were required to go off and work for a few years before they were allowed back for further study.

For eight years, therefore, she lived in a world that was almost uniquely privileged. That did not mean, however, that caution and care were not required: the forces of the state could turn vicious for no reason. Conditions in Larissa's time at the Academy and later at the Hermitage were nowhere near as dangerous as under high Stalinism – Geraldine Norman, in her fine history of the Hermitage, gives a list of staff arrested, persecuted or fired by the security apparatus, but there are relatively few names from the era of Stalin's successor, Nikita Khrushchev. There were nonetheless constant reminders of the past in the form of those returning from the prison camps. The Hermitage's director, Mikhail Artamonov, was known for accepting such people back, and there was a fair number of them, often in various states of trauma and ill-health.[2] One was Yury Ivanovich Kuznetsov, a specialist in Dutch drawings and another pupil of Larissa's own supervisor. Larissa remembered him as a wonderful, brilliant man, but his career at the Hermitage was blocked for years and he was kept in a subordinate position until the mid-1960s because of his war record. Kuznetsov had been called up, had fought against the Germans, and was taken prisoner. The regime disapproved strongly of people who were captured, rather than fighting to the death, so he had to spend the next twenty years under strict surveillance, and was banned from travelling abroad – a major problem for someone with his specialism. He was, however, a genial, knowledgeable colleague, 'a great chaser after women', and one of the first to be told of her marriage to Francis.

Another who was arrested and then returned during Larissa's time was Leonid Tarassuk, the Jewish keeper of arms and armour, who was a good friend and six years her senior. He was very erudite but 'an extraordinary character', even before he was arrested on arms charges. He was chronically indiscreet, a terrible womaniser, loved practical jokes (like getting hold of ten litres of vodka on expenses on the pretext of needing to pickle a dead curator) and was an expert fencer. He was sentenced to three years for hoarding weaponry. These were only old guns he discovered during an archaeological dig in the Caucasus and kept for himself, but he did have the habit of test-firing them into the ceilings of the Hermitage, and the authorities also had recordings of him making fun of the government.

His friends at the Hermitage collected money to employ the most famous lawyer in Moscow for his defence. There was a trial and the lawyer proved that there was nothing to accuse him of. All his conversations had occurred amongst relatives and the law permitted discussions with relatives about anything you wanted. It was only conversations outside of the family that could be condemned as propaganda. He should have been released but the KGB insisted. He went to prison for three years.

When Francis met him in 1965, Tarassuk claimed that Siberia was not so bad: 'treatment at first was harsh, afterwards all right – he had even, to some extent, thrived in the open air [and] was allowed to teach in a local school' (27 March 1965). But he still left Russia as quickly as he could, moving to Israel and the USA.

Larissa had no interest in politics and did not have any ambitions outside art history and conservatorship. Nor was there much of a family tradition of Party membership – her father refused to join until the war made it necessary, and her Uncle Yevgeny finally gave in and joined only in 1945, after the war had ended. Nikolai was an interesting case; Larissa could not remember him ever saying a good word about either the government or the Party, and even more than her, he loathed politics, politicians and the forces of the state in general. He was largely unmoved by the death of Stalin in 1953 – concerned about what it all meant, what would happen next, but, apart from that, not greatly disturbed. But when Khrushchev killed Stalinism itself in 1956 in a long, detailed, violent attack 'On the Cult of Personality and Its

Consequences', which laid out some of the horrors of the purges and the Gulag, Nikolai was shattered. This speech – dubbed the 'secret speech' in the West – did not remain secret for long, nor did Khrushchev intend it to. An edited version was circulated to local parties, news of it was swiftly leaked to Reuters, and the entire text rapidly made its way via Israel to the CIA, which promptly published it. It was designed to signal a break with the past and largely succeeded, but for many of the faithful, the remorseless detailing of the purges, failures and brutality was profoundly disillusioning, second only to the 1956 invasion of Hungary for weakening the hold Communism had both in the Soviet Union and in the West.

Larissa's father was so shocked he grew pale and had to be put to bed, where his wife and daughter maintained a vigil lest he die suddenly of a heart attack brought on by grief. Larissa found it all bemusing. As far as she was concerned, the only truly outrageous aspect of the message was the messenger. For Nikita Khrushchev to denounce Stalinism was the height of effrontery:

I was so indignant because most of the purges were in Ukraine and Khrushchev was the head of Ukraine and he was responsible for everything that happened there. Ukraine was the worst and Khrushchev was the one responsible for it. I wasn't surprised, but my father was. He was terribly anti-Soviet so I thought he knew it all.

Nikolai did – he had narrowly escaped execution himself, friends and colleagues had disappeared and been sent to labour camps, his brother had been arrested, he knew all too well how many lives had been lost during the war due to incompetence, corruption and indifference. Yet it seemed that he had managed to compartmentalise all of it as an aberration, not the true nature of the state he served. 'I realised then that underneath everything, he was a believer.'

Larissa was never a believer, but she was always patriotic. Not blindly so, but there was always a deep love of country that nothing could shake. She knew all of Russia's faults and was sometimes horrified by them, but also noted its positives – the education and cultural policies, the possibilities of genuine social mobility, the lack of materialism, the housing for the masses, all of which were considerably ahead of a country like Britain at the same time. So there was no strand of opposition in her approach, nor of opportunism. But sometimes her natural optimism was sorely tested. While in general she tried to avoid current affairs and politics, this became all but impossible as she grew into adulthood. As Francis was experiencing anti-Semitism in the army in 1947–8, so in Russia Stalin unleashed a wave of attacks on Jews which culminated in the 'Doctors' Plot' in January 1953. This was intended as a preliminary to a greater purge, which never happened because of Stalin's death two months later. It alleged that a group of doctors, most of whom were Jewish, had conspired under Western influence to murder members of the government.

Larissa remembered it as a hideous time: 'It was so awful that I thought of suicide. I couldn't stand it any longer. My father would come home and say that the workmen had hanged a Jewish engineer at his factory. It made people hate. It was really the most horrifying experience of my life.' Threatening groups surrounded her at bus stops asking if she was Jewish, and the way good friends might suddenly reveal a dark side of themselves frightened her even more: 'The worst thing was when suddenly an acquaintance said, "Perhaps these doctors were to blame?" If someone said something like that, then you knew that you could never trust them again.'

She was frightened above all because she had several Jewish friends, including her closest, Natasha Davidova, who survived unmolested because of her father, a captain in the navy. Filling out forms meant stating your nationality – Jewish counting as a nationality – but she was able to register herself as Russian because of his birth. Like Francis hiding his Judaism in the army, so Natasha did the same when applying to study biology at university. Larissa had no problems there, but she did have other reasons to be cautious. Natasha glossed over her mother, Larissa downplayed her father: 'I never wrote that I was a noble. I said my mother was a peasant.'

Natasha Davidova, *c.* 1956

But others were not so fortunate. Her school friend Irina Verblovskaya, also Jewish, fell in love with (and subsequently married) a young mathematician called Revolt Pimenov while studying history at university. As a mathematician, Pimenov did important work on the geometry of space-time, but he was also one of the earliest founders of the human rights movement in the Soviet Union and believed that the death of Stalin might open up the possibility of real reform. Along with a small group based in Leningrad, he began writing and distributing articles calling

Larissa and Mikhail Dobroklonsky, Lake Lagoda, *c.* 1960

for change. He was harassed for years but never picked up until 1957, after he denounced the invasion of Hungary, and the entire group was arrested. Pimenov was sentenced to ten years in jail and Irina, who had done little except be his girlfriend, got five, serving her entire sentence in a labour camp in Siberia. Pimenov continued to be harassed well into the 1970s, but Irina moved to Estonia and managed to avoid further difficulties, although her career as an academic was wrecked, her marriage disintegrated, and she worked as a tour guide in later life.

When Larissa began her fellowship, she was assigned to Mikhail Vasilivich Dobroklonsky (1886–1964), who became not only her supervisor, but her friend and protector.

He was the most extraordinary man ever. Before the Revolution, he was the secretary of Nicholas II … He should have been shot after the Revolution but he married a woman who was the daughter of a great Russian scientist … He was never arrested or persecuted. He taught at the Academy of Fine Arts. We absolutely adored him … He was often ill and whenever he was, we would collect money and buy him flowers and visit him. I became his 'Beloved Pupil'.

In addition to teaching at the Academy, Dobroklonsky was a curator in the department of Western Art at the Hermitage for decades and, when Larissa began her graduate work, he asked her to become his assistant. She had planned to write her dissertation on the seventeenth-century French engraver Jacques Callot, mainly in the hope that it would allow her to go and study in Paris, but he persuaded her to abandon that idea and write one on the eighteenth-century Venetian Giovanni Battista Tiepolo instead, although 'I never finished it because I was too busy amusing myself with my friends'.

Dobroklonsky needed help getting the Hermitage's drawings into order and decided that Larissa would be ideal to help him. 'One of the things about me was that I was from a noble family. That was rather important to him.' It was a Sisyphean task – even before the Revolution, the Hermitage had one of the largest collections of drawings in the world. After 1917, it doubled in size due to confiscations of private collections, and almost none of it was catalogued properly. Dobroklonsky started on the task of bringing order to the chaos in the 1920s, and was still at it, nowhere near finished, when he died. Larissa was a dedicated assistant – despite the prospect of Paris fading as a result – and spent much of her working life at the museum helping him. In return, she had full access to his conversation and immense knowledge. Dobroklonsky, because of his contacts and position as an Academician, had held on to his large pre-Revolution apartment in Leningrad and in addition had retained his personal art collection and library. All of this was put at Larissa's disposal, so she spent the better part of a decade learning to look, see and understand.

Quite what this entailed is easily underestimated, but working with drawings is often the most difficult and exacting of all tasks in art history. Unlike paintings, they are generally unsigned, and there is frequently no provenance, no way of knowing where they came from. Sometimes they are fully finished drawings, at other times mere sketches or doodles, a few lines on a piece of paper – although these, if properly identified, can prove to be the preliminary ideas for a painting and thus of enormous importance for understanding the evolution of more famous works. Often enough they are copies, sketches done by pupils or admirers that need to be distinguished from original works by a particular artist – and sometimes pupils could mimic their master so well their hands became almost identical. And, often, these drawings have their own beauty alongside their utility.

To penetrate their secrets, it is necessary to have technical skill – to recognise the type of paper, when it was made and where; what the ink was composed of; what type of brush or pencil was used. That is added to any documentary evidence that might exist, although with drawings this is often scanty. Taken together, these can give a hint of whether or not a drawing might be by a particular artist. But far more important is looking, knowing how an artist moved his hand over the paper, how he held the brush or pencil, how he thought when working out an idea. That is a level of knowledge that comes only from long, deep study, until you know the way the artist operated and can almost feel his hand at work.

That is what Larissa's fifteen years of training and work at the Hermitage gave her, and it was the area of art history where Francis was very much less adept: most of the works he studied were so well documented – in churches, museums or private collections with multiple records of their production and purchase – that he did not need expertise at that level. But it became Larissa's speciality, growing greater every year as she dug deeper into the Hermitage's resources, with Dobroklonsky on hand as teacher and guide.

Under his influence, she also learned Italian, although not well – 'I was incredibly lazy and never learnt Italian grammar. I could read but I could never write. When I came to Italy … my Italian was more or less non-existent.' But she knew enough to be able to claim she knew it and that, plus some familiarity with Venice itself, helped persuade the powers that be to send her to the Biennale. Thus, her intellectual journey paralleled Francis's emotional one: both began with a fascination for France and particularly Paris, and both gradually shifted over to a love of Italy and in particular Venice.

Dobroklonsky died in November 1964 aged 78, one of Larissa's last and greatest attachments to Russia, as by then her father was also dead. He was a widower and childless – all three sons were killed in the war – and had all but adopted Larissa: 'There was even gossip that I was his mistress. But he adored his wife and when she died he was incredibly miserable. He started drinking when she died.' It is unthinkable that she might have left the Soviet Union permanently while he was still alive. He left her all his books and his collection of pictures in his will, which caused some trouble getting them to England later on, and asked that, somehow, he be given a religious funeral.

This was all but impossible at this particular time; while tolerance, or intolerance, of religion rose and fell according to governmental whim, at that moment there was a high degree of repression. Dobroklonsky's coffin was put into a mortuary, to be buried the next day. Larissa, however, decided she had to honour his request. She organised some of the janitors and workmen from the Hermitage, commandeered a truck normally used for moving paintings, and drove to the hospital. There they announced they had come for the body to take it to the Academy for a civil service. Instead of doing that, they loaded the coffin into the back of the truck and drove it to a church on the other side of the city where Larissa had found a priest willing to officiate.

> If the truck had been stopped on the way to the church, we would have all been arrested. We put the body in the church and I asked his friends for money because the service cost an absolute fortune. But the choir and the special lights were everything that he wanted.

Once the service had been completed, her supervisor was loaded onto the truck once more and taken to the Academy. 'I drove across the city sitting on my supervisor's coffin. I had no idea how I would have explained this if we'd been stopped by the police. I was quite terrified the whole time.'

## Larissa: School, Academy, Hermitage, 1944–1962

The concentration on Italian art and, in particular, Venetian drawings put Larissa in an ideal position to be Dobroklonsky's professional heir, and when she was given a permanent position at the Hermitage at the end of her scholarship, she moved into her new role with little fuss. Getting such a job at the age of 26 was a remarkable achievement, and even more remarkable for a woman. The war was partly responsible. The carnage had more than decimated the population of young men. The best estimates are that nearly 36 per cent of all men between the ages of 18 and 34 died. Leningrad was particularly badly hit: due to the siege a third of a civilian population of near 3.4 million died and many of the 1.4 million who were evacuated took years to return. While before the war the Soviet Union was theoretically more ready than most countries to give opportunities to women, men would still do better in the search for good jobs. But the war meant that there weren't enough men available, and even some of those who survived were so traumatised that they were incapable of working. Larissa recalled that some of the students at the Academy 'came from the front and weren't normal':

Occasionally, they would go to the hospital to treat their nerves. Sometimes I would be sent to give lectures to them in the hospital and I have never experienced such extraordinary ordeals. They were so nervous and would listen to you with such feeling that you felt inspired. But when you finished, they would ask the most absurd questions ...

The Hermitage was, and is, an extraordinary institution. The largest museum in the world, its holdings come from the old Imperial collections, works requisitioned from private collections after the Revolution, and still more looted in various wars. Its prominence made it noticeable, but also gave it a certain degree of

117

protection, and its self-assurance generated a spirit of independence that made it often resistant to the pressures of the outside world. Moreover, it was in Leningrad, which tended towards a similarly superior and dismissive view of the rest of the country. The protection it enjoyed was not at all perfect; orders that could not be circumvented and arrests of employees were both frequent under Stalinism. But the museum survived surprisingly well as an autonomous body, not least because of its success in appointing directors from the inside – Artamonov and later the two Piotrovskys – who mingled a canny ability at bureaucratic politics with a true devotion to the institution they ran.[3] This success – Artamonov was appointed in 1951, and the younger Piotrovsky is still (as of 2024) in post – ensured nearly three-quarters of a century of stability despite remarkably disruptive times.

Still, the odd side of Soviet life did occasionally cause disruption to the daily regime at both the museum and the Academy. One such was compulsory potato-picking, although Larissa quickly managed to get into the position of choosing others to go on this universally disliked show of solidarity, rather than go herself. But as a student it was a regular event every year:

It was a long way away, about eight hours by train. We had to dig potatoes for a week. Once it started snowing on the second day and never stopped. We had students from socialist countries, such as Hungary and Romania, who were sent as well … when they arrived, they said that the conditions were awful and that they had it much better at home. They were stunned, as they thought that Russia was more advanced.

Another duty was the annual medical competition, to keep people in practice for giving first aid in case of another war. Larissa and some of her friends were selected by the Hermitage authorities because they had so obstinately refused to do any of the other patriotic duties that came up. While the other team – from a factory – came dressed in uniform and ready to compete properly, the one from the Hermitage arrived in their most elegant clothes, and the keeper of Chinese art tried to skew the results by seducing the judge. They were not very good and manifestly refused to take it at all seriously, but still did well because, when asked how to treat a man with a hand wound, they all looked blank. The opposing team – 'completely uneducated; you have no idea' – recommended putting a tourniquet around his neck and pulling tight. Doing nothing was considered safer than actively killing the patient and the Hermitage team was awarded the gold medal.

The museum also had a resident KGB officer, his job being to sniff out unhealthy opinions and subversive thoughts, although in practice this meant little more than collecting gossip. It was not an important position, and so tended to be given to low-grade officers, unsuitable for more important tasks because of health, age or lack of intelligence. The officer for much of Larissa's time was not particularly agreeable but was not considered very dangerous either – no one in the museum was purged or disciplined through his work while she was there. His job consisted of summoning individuals to his office for a chat every now and then and trying to get them to criticise colleagues. Institutional solidarity, however, blunted the effectiveness of this approach. Larissa said only pleasant things even about those she detested, and most others did the same. There was no advantage for anyone to provide such information and a very substantial downside: gaining a reputation as a KGB snitch, which some certainly did, could damage your progress quite effectively if colleagues withdrew their trust. However, although the officer was not especially skilled or dedicated to his work, they understood that it was necessary to feed him enough information to keep his own superiors happy. Once she had joined the Party, Larissa was often brought in to escort dignitaries and visitors around the museum, and happily provided details of what they said – summarising conversations with Alexei Kosygin, the then Foreign Minister, when she gave him a tour of the department of Western art in 1964. It did no harm to anyone who mattered to her and made the KGB officer look good.

The situation changed somewhat when he was replaced, shortly before Larissa left, by a much younger and more personable man. 'He was so handsome. Marta fell hopelessly in love with him.' This one was intelligent, was foreign posting quality, and began to make inroads into office solidarity through sheer charm. Fortunately, an explanation for his being there in a position way below his level soon became apparent – he died of cirrhosis of the liver before he could do too much damage.

Larissa applied to join the Party in 1962 and, after a period of candidacy, was accepted before she left for Venice and the Biennale. Why she decided to do this is unclear: she was certainly never a doctrinaire Marxist, and membership was not obligatory either. At one stage she said it was required so she could go to Venice, at others that she was pushed into it by workers at the Hermitage – sweepers and cleaners – who wanted a friendly voice inside the Party and on the directing committee. She does seem to have applied well before the prospect of going to the Biennale appeared, however, although it is possible she would not have been chosen had she not been at least in the process of becoming a Party member.

As far as Larissa was concerned, membership of the Party offered few advantages, certainly none that matched the patronage of her supervisor. It also brought many disadvantages, above all work that she found tiresome. On her return from Venice at the end of 1962 she was put on the Party committee which supervised Hermitage policy and found this fairly interesting. Other work was more onerous: pay at the Hermitage was poor, and despite the best efforts of the director, the government refused to increase it. Instead, Artamonov relaxed the rules governing outside work, so that employees could add to their income by taking jobs on the side. The condition was that this could not interfere with official duties, and Larissa was put in charge of the committee that issued the certificate confirming this was the case, without which it was illegal to receive payment. She certified everything without asking too many questions, but it was time-consuming, nonetheless.

There were lengthy and tedious sessions where Party members were summoned to analyse ideological niceties of Marxism–Leninism as it applied to museums – desperately boring but which she had to appear interested in. She had to volunteer for tasks the Party considered important, such as getting out the vote for elections in her neighbourhood, which was hard as most knew full well that the result had already been decided. All this was burdensome, and not even very advantageous socially, as most of her friends tended to belong to the faction at the Hermitage which disliked the Party and tended to be suspicious of its members.

Apart from the occasional need to be careful in conversation, Larissa loved every moment of her time at the Hermitage – the work, the colleagues, the collections themselves. It was the perfect job, not least because the museum operated in a way which allowed its curators considerable autonomy in their own domains and she could decide for herself what to do. Nominally the work was nine to five, six days a week, with only two weeks' holiday, but this was hard to enforce:

I could walk there in forty minutes but I usually overslept so
... I was always late. Then they introduced a scheme where
you had a number which you would put in a box when you
arrived. I would ask people to put mine in the box for me.
They couldn't control us and the Hermitage was so huge
that it was impossible to find anyone.

***

As Larissa's period as a student came to an end and she began
to work properly, her parents decided it was high time she got
married. She did have a lover, a colleague from the Chinese
department of the Hermitage called Evgeny Lubo-Lesnichenko:
'It was love at first sight. I went completely mad.' There were
problems, however: 'The main disadvantage for me was that he
was married and had two children ... he was the most unfaithful
man one could imagine.' Vera did suggest allowing him to move
in, but he would occasionally bring other women with him, and
the relationship turned into simple, safer friendship.

Larissa wooing *c.* 1959

So Larissa's parents did as all responsible parents would and cast around among their acquaintance for a suitable match. Through friends in Moscow, they hit on the perfect man in Alexander Bakhchiev, a talented young pianist and recent graduate from the Moscow Conservatoire. He was the same age, came with good credentials, was reputed to be perfectly sweet, and there seemed to be an obvious commonality of interest. Both sets of parents were so delighted at their stroke of genius that they all but started organising the wedding. Alexander's put him on the train to Leningrad so that the couple could get better acquainted, accept the ideal nature of the match, and set matters rolling. After that, everything would proceed straightforwardly.

But you can lead a horse to water. By Larissa's account, Bakhchiev was handsome, intelligent, kindly, talented and a good man. And after a few days with him she went to the railway station and bought him a one-way ticket to Moscow with instructions not to come back. 'He was so boring, I can't tell you. All he did was talk about piano technique.' Her decision was so absolute that Bakhchiev rejected his parents' urging that he return to Leningrad to have another go, and the matter was eventually dropped. But they remained good friends – he ultimately married a musicologist and had a distinguished career as both a concert pianist and as a teacher, and Larissa was fond of his daughter.

Whatever she might have been looking for, a handsome, pleasant and accomplished musician was not it. Nor was the man she married in 1959 who, at least initially, she detested. This was Viktor Mikhailov, an ex-submariner then teaching at the Naval Academy in Leningrad and a distant relation of her supervisor. They had got off to a bad start when he said that he didn't like ballet, and she told him that, in that case, he was an idiot. He was quite smitten by this forthrightness, and pursued her:

His passion was his boat and he spent his whole time in a yacht club. The Naval Academy had a trip each year and he proposed that I come with him. I wasn't busy at the time so I said, 'Why not?' We went and we immediately ran into terrible trouble. We lost the other boats and became completely independent and travelled from one island to another. Gradually, we became lovers and later it grew into a nice relationship.

The Naval Academy seems to have raised no objections to someone taking one of their boats on a private holiday without permission, and the relationship which began on it developed sufficiently for the pair to marry in late 1959. Quite why, Larissa could not remember. Certainly, she could not recall loving him particularly, but getting married, and to someone in the military, did at least calm her parents down for a while. He was, in addition, perfectly pleasant – generous, good-hearted and a loyal husband, even if, as it turned out, he was not at all a faithful one. They were married for nearly three years, but he was never a particularly important part of her life; they had nothing in common and never even lived together. In her vast collection of photographs, which contains images of every friend, acquaintance, colleague and relative, there is not a single one of her husband. Any prospect of a happy union was made more difficult by the unusual nature of property relations in the Soviet Union, which did more to take the romance out of marriage (and depress the catastrophically low birth rate) than anything else:

All the property belonged to the state. Each individual had the right to eight square metres unless you had a certain privilege. You were more or less attached to where you lived. The police registered you there. If I married you and you came to live with us, you would have equal rights to everyone else.

This meant that if the marriage broke up, then either you would be stuck with your now estranged spouse, or he might leave and pass his share on to someone else. The prospect did not meet with the approval of Larissa's mother, who had endured having her apartment subdivided and filled with strangers when Larissa's uncle had moved out and his share of the apartment was assigned to a drunkard. So Viktor lived with his aunt, an invalid who was frequently taken off to a dacha by other members of his family. This meant that he had the space to himself much of the year, and Vera could relax. But the aunt no more wanted Larissa moving in than Vera wanted Viktor doing so.

When Larissa went to Italy for the Biennale, Viktor began an affair with her best friend, Natasha Davidova, who came and nervously confessed on her return. Larissa was less upset than was anticipated, possibly because she had herself by that time started her affair with Francis: 'Natasha wanted him … and I told her she could have him.'

She kept the friend and gave away the husband, whom she swiftly divorced – a procedure which in Russia at the time was extremely simple as long as no property or children were involved. It was a sound decision: she had been friends with Natasha for years, who was part of the close group that met several times a week. Losing her would have broken up her entire social circle; losing her husband, in contrast, was a bit of a relief, and made no difference to her life at all. Besides, any awkwardness did not last long: he continued to have affairs and Natasha soon dispatched him as well.

# 6

# Francis: Italy, 1952–1962

*Becoming an Art Historian – Archives – A Syphilitic Duke –*
*Brothels – The Occult – Puppets – Landscape*

By the time he went to Italy in 1952, Francis was an experienced traveller, far more capable of making his own way. He had a topic and sufficient money, but this time could not call on family connections – few Russian exiles ended up in Italy and, as it was not a great centre for ballet either, neither of his parents had any contacts there.[1] He found a room with a family, the Palmas, at 90 viale Angelico, a mile north of the Vatican, which provided him with accommodation, food and a great deal of entertainment. He also found a small supplementary source of income by teaching English to 'the Count': 'rather anti-patico, didn't offer me a ciga-rette, ask how I like Rome etc. Whole thing conducted on very business-like terms, and he's paying 800 l. an hour for 2 hours a week. He wants to translate golf papers' (21 February 1952). It was a wonderful period in Francis's life. Tolerably well-funded, he perfected his Italian, basked in the freedom that being out of England always gave him, and laid out the framework of the historical approach which shaped his career and the study of art history.

He arrived in Italy a self-educated amateur with no formal training in a field which scarcely existed. England at the time did not produce professionally trained art historians; most came to the subject through connoisseurship, working with pictures themselves – either in museums, auction houses or, often enough, by studying their family's own collections. The only place in the country where it was possible to study art as a subject properly was at the Courtauld Institute in London, and that was only founded in 1931. But while the Courtauld largely managed to avoid becoming a finishing school for the wealthy, it was very much designed to train people for the art trade. Only with the arrival in the 1930s of the remarkable German-Jewish refugees – Rudolf Wittkower, Nikolaus Pevsner, Ernst Gombrich – did art history get an injection of Germanic rigour and begin to form into an academic discipline.

Little of this, however, had penetrated to Cambridge, and those intellectual currents which had made the fifty-mile jour-ney north made little impression on Francis. He had switched to English in his last year but found that, despite his love of literature, the subject left him cold. English was also a relatively new field as an academic subject. It had appeared as a sort of poor man's Classics at the end of the nineteenth century, and only established itself properly within the universities after the First World War. By the late 1940s it was triumphant, but Francis was not convinced; he doubted the absolutist and politicised views that the founders of the discipline espoused and took an instant dislike to the subject's savage and doctrinaire guru, F. R. Leavis: 'a small, mean-looking man [with] an adenoidal, unculti-vated voice ...' (11 October 1950). Still, he decided he wanted to continue in academia for a while, if only because he could think of nothing else to do, and it was Nikolaus Pevsner who gave him the idea of looking at the particular styles of art and architecture associated with the Jesuit Order in the seventeenth century – a topic which appealed primarily because it meant he would have to go and live in Rome.

While he had been looking at paintings for years, he was still quite conventional in his opinions. His strength lay in this weakness, however. He felt that the connoisseurship approach – who painted what and when – was self-indulgent, that the iconographic analysis of the Germans was too abstract, and he thoroughly disliked the ideologically driven social history approach that was dominated by Marxism. That left his own interests and knowledge of people. He came to his project as a *tabula rasa* and began to read documents in the archives with few preconceived ideas. His first great discovery was that his topic did not exist – there was no 'Jesuit style'. This realisation came not from the ideas of leading academics, but from casual conversations with priests who knew their churches, and archivists who had actually read some of the documents: 'he threw one efficient spanner in my works by pointing out that, of course, often it was a private family, rather than the church authorities, who chose the picture for individual chapels' (9 March 1952).

In fact, he swiftly realised that the notoriously severe and austere Jesuits ended up with all those extravagant and gaudy churches and paintings not because they wanted them particularly, but because that was what their patrons wanted to give them, and they were too weak and needy to say no. Bit by bit, archive by archive, letter by letter, he teased out the delicate filaments of a complex network of connections between cardinals, nobles and collectors, painters, sculptors and architects, in Rome and Venice and provincial cities, tracing how ideas spread, tastes changed, commissions were handed out, and reputations made or destroyed.

Everything that interested him in his own life was brought into play – he read letters and journals, was intrigued by personalities, understood instinctively how patronage and networking functioned, sensed the importance of friendship, rivalry and admiration in making ideas and styles develop. In the archives he discovered 'a whole new world, whose inhabitants so resembled my own friends, colleagues, rivals and enemies that I felt I could easily understand them ...'[2] Equally, he used his tendency to observe himself to good effect, and blended the quite mechanical issue of artistic production with the question of taste – why are some works accepted as masterpieces, others dismissed as trash? Why do styles and artists go in and out of favour? This problem had first come to mind in Ely Cathedral on a wet winter's day in 1950:

I was horrified to find myself admiring some stained glass windows and then, as soon as I learnt that they were modern, liking them far less ... This set me thinking on taste, and art appreciation generally ... there can be no objective standards in criticism ... good taste is merely what a whole lot of people whom one respects like. What is interesting is why people should like certain things ... (15 February 1950)

Curiously – or revealingly – four days later he could approvingly describe a friend in the fashion he had just decided was useless: 'He has excellent and personal taste in all the arts ...' (19 February 1950). But it is interesting that this idea – the central concept of his approach to history – arose out of a meticulous scrutiny of himself, his own thoughts and reactions, rather from more abstract theorising. It was an issue which wouldn't leave him alone – 'The altar [in San Giovanni in Laterano] I thought looked rather like the Albert Memorial – but I have since heard that it is very fine Gothic – and feel rather ashamed' (1 March 1952).

Many of the archives he needed were scattered around the country; some books were to be found in the library of the British School at Rome or the Biblioteca Nazionale, but the friends who initially sustained him mainly came through the British Council, which was then the unofficial club of the educated Briton abroad. It had been founded in the 1930s as a response to the rise of fascism and was repurposed after 1945 as a response to the spread of Communism. In its heyday it was an eccentric organisation, often staffed by very odd people doing their best to cooperate with, and rival, better-funded organisations representing other countries – the French had their Maisons françaises, the Germans the Goethe Instituts, the Americans an extensive network of libraries, while the Russians had the (cheaper but more widespread) national Communist parties to spread the word for them. All were supposed to propagate knowledge about, and the languages of, their respective countries: they were part of the first culture war of the modern era, but conducted themselves with decorum and civility, and with unlikely foot soldiers. Many a novelist came to regard a British Council book tour with something approaching terror, and legends abounded of empty meeting halls, books that failed to arrive and even authors who were never seen again. Francis himself did a four-week lecture tour in 1958; he enjoyed the travel but found the experience dispiriting when he realised that the audiences generally came merely to practise their English and were largely uninterested in what he was saying.

For the most part, the Council conducted its campaigns through English lessons, lectures on Shakespeare, drinks to celebrate the King's birthday, and cream teas in the blistering Mediterranean heat. But it also acted as an employment exchange for itinerant English students, a way to meet fellow exiles, a parking place for mid-level civil servants to serve out their time before retirement, and – by repute at least – was a favourite of MI6, which was said to pack off its spies to unlikely places under cover of being librarians or language teachers. In Francis's time, the head of the Council in Rome was Brigadier Brian Kennedy-Cooke, an amiable man who had spent most of his Colonial Office career on postings in the Horn of Africa and was a noted authority on Sudanese botany.[3] He would invite suitable young men for Sunday lunch – fire blazing whatever the weather outside – in a manner which reminded Francis of similar hospitality from his old headmaster.

It was the British Council that provided the golfing count, and in addition gave Francis the chance to earn a little money delivering lectures to English-language students in Tuscany during his first summer there. This was erratically organised: when one teacher was too hungover to teach coherently, he shooed all the pupils onto the grass outside the villa and played them records over a loudspeaker of Laurence Olivier's speeches from *Henry V*, which echoed over the Tuscan countryside in a manner that Francis found strangely evocative. He soon realised that his own lectures on art history were so complicated that none of the pupils could understand a word he was saying, but he carried on regardless and was complimented by both organisers and pupils for his efforts. Perhaps more importantly, the Council provided companionship, particularly a friendly young woman from Cumbria called Meriel Stocker – 'I like her more than any girl I've ever met' (25 March 1952) – who was his constant companion throughout his stay. A second was Lyndall Hopkinson, an emotionally complex woman who had run away to Rome to escape an overzealous suitor and her famously wayward novelist mother.[4] These two, plus another art historian called Willy Mostyn-Owen – who had money, a car and was then working as an amanuensis to the great connoisseur Bernard Berenson – were his closest English contacts. In addition, he got to know Italians, especially the family he lodged with, and later Enzo Crea, a publisher who remained a close friend for the

Francis: Italy, 1952–1962

Meriel Stocker (*l*) and (*?*) Lyndall Hopkinson (*r*), Umbria, 1952

Enzo Crea, Francis, Larissa and Sandro Marabottini, Rome, 1966

rest of his life, the increasingly impoverished journalist Umberto Morra and the historian and collector Sandro Marabottini.

Above all, he got to know Italy – the entire country this time, as his knowledge of France was always more limited and for a long time mainly confined to Paris. His expeditions justified by the search for archives, he went to Turin, Milan, Venice and all the major cities of Northern Italy; to Assisi, Perugia, Siena and Florence in the centre; to Naples and Palermo in the south. He stayed with contacts or in cheap hotels, working assiduously when the archives were open and sometimes when they were not: in Verona in 1957, he had a heavy drinking session to win over an archivist and 'later that night we went up to the untouched archives, and banging the huge folders onto the rickety floor to shake off some of the thick clouds of dust, we looked in vain for the will of Marshall Schulenburg by the light of a sort of miner's lamp ...' (8 September 1957).

Doing research then was very different: no computers, and often enough not even a catalogue or card index: 'In the morning to the Vatican ... looked round the library, idiotically uncatalogued' (14 February 1952). Access frequently meant having to tap into the memory of historians and archivists who might – or might not – go off and find material, depending on their mood and the proximity of lunch time: 'went to call on Professore Hass. Had some difficulty in getting hold of him, as he apparently cuts off the electricity when he goes out, and forgets to turn it on again' (5 March 1952). Even the major institutions were difficult to use: 'looked in at the Biblioteca Nazionale. Getting a book here is rather on the principle of a lucky dip at a children's party. The catalogue seems to be 20 years' out of date, and hasn't really made up its mind whether it's indexing books by subject or by author' (26 January 1952). There were no passes, no controls, no security and an often erratic supply of material: 'I spent virtually the whole day working in the archives in conditions like those of a Marx brothers film …' (Vicenza, 8 September 1957). Sometimes archivists could be deliberately obstructive, occasionally enormously helpful – as in the case of Maria Francesca Tiepolo in Venice, whose knowledge of eighteenth-century art was prodigious, not least because her family had produced so much of it.[5]

Mostly, he learned his business: trailing round museum after museum, church after church, noting down everything of interest at a time when there was little recent scholarship to use as a starting point. Indeed, his most useful book was a 1906 Baedeker guide, which he found to be more serious – as less aimed at the superficial modern tourist – than the post-war *Guide Bleu* he bought on his arrival. His appetite was phenomenal, but sometimes even he overdosed: 'it was a killing visit; after about the 10,000th picture I began to hate art …' (Venice, 5 August 1956). Equally, his commitment would occasionally flag: 'Suddenly felt that all academic research is absolutely pointless, and why don't I go and drown myself' (13 February 1952).

He entered a Felliniesque world and, because he had a good eye for the odd and unusual, his diaries are liberally sprinkled with characters who would make excellent cameos in a movie – the landlady in a tremble of pleasure because a *contessa* turned up to her mother's funeral; the kept woman living alone in a grandiose villa with only a tortoise and a snake for company;[6] the Mussolini-loving maid who served a dessert made with animal blood which sent him to bed with cramps for two days; the girl who fainted on hearing that he was an atheist; the aged *principessa* who hit her husband on the head with a crucifix as he sat in the bath 'because he refused to grant her conjugal rights' (8 September 1957). Or the 'syphilitic Duke' in Gallese, near Viterbo:

head grotesquely twisted, accompanied by a servant to see that he doesn't fall ... he told me that he didn't think it would be possible to visit the palace as his wife had gone away and taken the keys: 'She just leaves me without telling me where she is going or how long for,' he explained pathetically. 'She steals from me all the time.' There are some curious frescoes in a frieze around the walls ... but the Duke was only interested in telling us (which he did three times) about the bathroom which his father had installed ... 'So convenient,' he kept on explaining as if talking of some fabulous discovery ... At one point, he gripped Luigi [Salerno] by the arm and begged for a cigarette but was cruelly stopped by the servant.[7] At a later stage Luigi managed to smuggle one to him, explaining to me afterwards that it might hasten his death. For Luigi is craftily waiting for the break up of the family and the dispersal of the pictures which is then due to take place – and this added one more turn of the screw to a situation that was already macabre and grotesque enough for a 19th century novel. (17 September 1962)

Alongside the individuals are the general glimpses of the Italians en masse – the 'church troglodytes, those curious old women, who seem to be buried in the darkest chapels always, and who mutter furiously when one disturbs them by looking at the pictures.' Then there were the squares 'full of charming life – little children clinging on to the robes of the Franciscan monks, the men peeing against the walls, or playing cards in the piazzas, standing around doing nothing' (5 March 1952).

And there were his trips to brothels – often, but not always, as an observer of local life:

Curiously enough, rather like English pubs, these close at 11.30, so we had to be quick. The first one was almost exactly like the waiting room at a National Health Service hospital. On the way in, we had to show our 'documents' to a tooth-less, hunchback hag. Then into a large spare room, crowded with men, mostly young, all smoking, and mostly knowing each other; among them were two carabinieri in brilliant uniform ... Every few minutes a girl, dressed in evening clothes would come down some stairs, and stand on a raised platform ... Sometimes one of the men would go up to her at once, and they would go up the stairs together ...

I was completely staggered. The whole thing seemed quite bewildering ... Practically all Italian boys of every class have their first sexual experience in these brothels ... Admission is at the age of 18; consequently, a boy is taken there by his friends virtually on his birthday. I asked about confession. Apparently, the priest says 'Well, try and go only the bare minimum number of times.'

They very rarely go alone – almost always in groups. They then are able to maintain a much more valuable type of comradeship than in England ... Any girl they go out with is never interfered with. Everyone expects to marry a virgin ... The girls themselves I imagine are utterly, irretrievably ruined like so much rubbish in a dustbin. (20 January 1952)

The visit says as much about him as it does about Italy in the early 1950s. Most of the description focuses not on the prostitutes, but rather on the male sociability involved, and to be included in a masculine activity was indeed the reason he went in the first place. But in his equally brief foray to the Sphinx in Paris in 1946, he spent most of his time engaging the women there in conversation, trying to figure out their lives. Although that was undoubtedly the slumming of a curious late adolescent, he was clearly far more interested in the girls as people than as bodies: while he had the money and opportunity to go upstairs with one had he really wanted to, he instead sat and talked to them about their thoughts, hopes and ambitions, not about their trade. The anonymity, the completely depersonalised nature of what he witnessed in Rome – mixed with the very different but equally depersonalised idea of what a girl one might marry must be like – completely repelled him. For his part, he could not avoid considering the impact on the inmates, which concerned his fellows not at all. So, he could observe, but not readily take part. The visit gave him a lot to think about, but his response was ultimately rejection: whatever he was looking for, this was not it.

Finally there was politics, with Italians, then as now, always ready to take their views onto the streets, with warnings of dire consequences: 'People also talk … of a possible coup d'état … but as I have heard this raised every time there has been any trouble in Italy over the last 10 years I don't believe it any longer' (10 July 1964). In the early 1950s Trieste was the main focus of discontent – the region had been divided up after the war as a temporary measure and there were arguments among the occupying powers about whether Italy or Yugoslavia would ultimately be given control; inevitably this became an aspect of the Cold War more generally. As the occupiers haggled, Italians became as indignant as Yugoslavs about the claims of the other, and this produced regular marches through the streets, all of which Francis enjoyed watching: 'Slogans everywhere, of course, and very large crowds in the piazza in front of the station; traffic held up – "students" rushing around, and processions. Nothing much actually happening, and things seemed slightly unreal …' (25 March 1952).

The sense of theatre he picked up was powerful; Italy was awash with conspiracy theories, as it was when I lived there myself in the 1970s: the country pioneered the post-truth society which has since spread around the world. The difference between then and now – another break with the past – is that then many of the most convoluted and seemingly ridiculous rumours turned out to be true. The secret services were indeed infiltrated by the far right and involved in terrorist attacks on their own citizens; the CIA really was funding them; many in the government were very much beholden to the Mafia and the Vatican, sometimes both at the same time; and a shadowy Masonic lodge did tie organised crime, Church, government and high finance together to keep a tight grip on the country.

In the dreamlike, surreal world of post-war Italy, what Italians liked to call 'the occult' existed, and official accounts were far too dull to compete with a more entertaining story: 'Ugo Spirito strongly supports the current delightful rumour … that the current Pope has a mistress in Milan' (14 September 1964).[8] Rather than combatting the innumerable, and often contradictory tales swirling around the country, Francis realised that the Italian response was to settle back and enjoy the show, content to offer commentaries from the sidelines as long as it made no difference to their lives: 'The Italians – or at any rate the Romans – don't care a hoot for anything that doesn't immediately concern them' (4 March 1953).

In this period, he transferred his affections definitively from France to Italy. He continued to love Paris 'despite the fact that the people are not friendly … I still find Paris the most beautiful and exciting place in the world …' (13 July 1964), but realised that he was rarely able to become close to the French. Indeed, he made no long-term friends there, but in Italy he fell in love with the people as much as the place, finding a constant satisfaction in the friends he made, in transient conversations with total strangers, and through simply observing life from the vantage point of a café terrace, a train or a bus.

He fell into a country that was rapidly changing, far faster than England had ever done: post-war reconstruction, and the influx of American money into Europe through the Marshall Plan, turbo-charged economic and social change and led to what in France was called 'les trente glorieuses' and in Italy the 'miracolo economico'. The signs of change were everywhere, even in small parts of Sicily: 'Ragusa has a rather simpatico character, though it may well be ruined now that oil has been discovered nearby. Already there are Americans, Germans and Anglo-Iranians in the town, and more are expected' (25 February 1953). But he caught much of the old world as it faded away, sometimes knowingly, at other times not. He and his friends treated their pains with laudanum, that potent mixture of opium and alcohol which had kept everyone in Europe from babies to monarchs drugged up to the eyeballs for centuries. Dealing with toothache required courage, alcohol and a willing-ness to engage in long conversations: 'to the dentist again – a nice chap; he insisted on hearing all about the National Health Service in between burning my gums with a sinister electric instrument' (16 February 1952).

Checking into a hotel could be equally perilous: 'an extraordi-nary and horrifying room ... the sheets looked damp and dirty, there was a half-full chamber pot ... a filthy basin outside in the passage, the lavatory a disaster ... but there was no alternative' (26 March 1953). Even staying with friends could test the nerves: 'an endless amount of the most unsuitable food and drink imagi-nable and a "lavatory" so appalling as to make one constipated for life' (26 July 1953). He felt the change in his own reactions: on a trip to Anagni, to the south-east of Rome, he noted that all the women wore brilliantly coloured clothes. 'This is the only place I have yet come across where people seem to wear a genuine folk costume. It is genuine, but, of course, it looks fake' (13 January 1953).

Only when he went south, on a grand trip to Sicily in 1953 with his friend Willy Mostyn-Owen, did he properly see an unchanged country, as much of the island seemed scarcely to have entered the nineteenth century, let alone the twentieth. In March and April they set out in Mostyn-Owen's Jaguar into a land where the arrival of any car brought out every child on the streets to watch, and where the sole sources of income were 'olives, the sea and foreigners' (11 March 1953). It was desperately poor; the only place he visited in the 1950s which was even more immiserated was Portugal. In the cathedral of Catania 'a number of people were getting ready for a sermon. They provided a horrible, frightening picture of misery and degradation ... most of them stooping, crippled or paralysed ... we now reached the lowest point of our journey ...' (17 March 1953).

Still, he found Sicily 'everything I had hoped it would be, a land of dreams come true' (29 March 1953). They had moved from the Italy of Fellini to the Italy of *The Leopard*, often staying with contacts, many from the decayed aristocracy who lived in crumbling palazzi, eating poor food in dark and freezing rooms with silent, pious daughters in attendance. He even encountered Giuseppe Tomasi di Lampedusa himself, although as the novel was not published until 1958, Francis found his Baltic-German wife to be more strikingly memorable:

The room was large, lined with books, in semi-darkness, and though it was warm outside, very cold. I could smell the nauseating fumes of the inevitable oil stove. There were three women there, all wrapped up in as many clothes as they could lay their hands on. The most prominent was the Princess [of Lampedusa], a gigantic woman, heavily draped in furs, which made her size almost unmanageable ... the prince, looking like a self-satisfied and elderly Milan businessman, but evidently rather intelligent, sat, looking rather lost and very silent, in the corner. We drank sherry ... and listened to the Princess explaining to us all about world politics: the whole of the Russian government is made up of foreigners – Jews, Georgians, etc. Not one of our more successful visits. (Monreale, 4 April 1953)

It was a land where the streets were still covered in extracts from Mussolini's speeches while 'the offices of the Monarchist party which seem to be everywhere make a change after the Communism of the North' (27 March 1953). Worse, the weather was dreadful, the incessant rain made more depressing by the fact that they were told every night that it would be a lovely day tomorrow.

But they saw wonders – not just the inevitable churches and monasteries and museums, but little glimpses of something special that was passing away. One afternoon in Acireale, north of Catania, they saw a boy carrying a puppet and asked him about it. He led them to a building and showed them some more, 'all in armour or brilliantly coloured costume, representing knights and ladies from Ariosto, Tasso and Legends of the Crusades, each nearly three foot high'. An unshaven man came in and said that he was 'very honoured to meet us'. This turned out to be Emanuele Macrì, one of the last great puppeteers of the old tradition, who knew the ancient stories by heart, and who gave a performance just for them:

A battle between a Christian and a pagan. This was one of the most enjoyable dramatic performances I have ever seen. The characters entered with a superb flourish; a leap through the air and a wide gesture before he [sic] settled. And then the battle itself: utterly stylised so that it was nearer ballet than theatre, the characters flung their bodies backwards and forwards rhythmically, clashing swords, until the pagan, his head cut off in one superb blow, lay crumpled on the floor.[9] (18 March 1953)

Everything Francis valued merged in this one experience, and his description blended them together – the ballet, the artistry, the stories, the Spanish-Arabic music, all became elements in one overall account: 'the marvellous colour of the costumes and the gleam of the golden armour, as fine as anything devised by Bakst ... the wonderfully easy, noble stylised gestures ... with a little practice, one could easily pick up this new, more spacious and eloquent language'. And holding it all together was Macrì himself, who 'seemed to grow in size, until he turned into a larger-than-life Dickens character ... for us the enjoyment came from the way he himself lived the legends, the dramatic way in which

Acireale puppet theatre: postcard bought by Francis in March 1953 and signed by Emanuele Macrì

he told them ...' This tendency to merge his responses to life and art grew to the point that, when he wrote the following day of Militello in Sicily 'swarming with grotesques ...' (19 March 1953), it is not immediately apparent whether he was referring to the carvings on the walls or to the inhabitants.

The same mixing appears in his response to the Italian land-scape, something he rarely bothered with elsewhere – there are few descriptions of either the English or French countryside, for example. But Italy was different:

At first the countryside seemed drab, almost Belgian – but after about an hour it had grown on me, almost by magic – slow, undulating hills, a few rising darker and more sharply in the distance – a few, very few, trees and odd houses dotted around. But it didn't really look like Claude, except for the golden light, which was indescribably beautiful and by some curious alchemy, transformed the countryside ... (21 February 1952)

This appreciation was formed above all by driving around the countryside outside Rome on the back of an old but functional Vespa driven by his friend Sandro Marabottini – after a year with the Palmas, he had moved with the historian Luigi Salerno to live in a flat on the Aventine Hill which Marabottini had bought but could not afford. He then accompanied his new friend, also an art historian, on expeditions to investigate the region. Marabottini remembered the period as producing a pleasurable fusion of art and geography:

if we followed the wide bends of the Tiber, that was Poussin's promenade; the Soratte, high and sometimes on the summit dusted with white snow, rather than through the classic filter of Horace, appeared to us as the background of a Dughet, and walking along the wide valleys that descend from Castel Giuliano to Cerveteri, populated by herds of horses and cattle, we walked in the blue and luminous depths of Claude Lorrain's canvases.[10]

Later, and whenever Francis could latch on to someone who could drive, these trips extended across Italy more generally, taking in not only the central part of Italy from Rome to Bologna, but also Sicily and the Adriatic coast. All of these trips were both satisfying and occasionally alarming. Driving on the streets of Rome on an underpowered Vespa, often after an excessively good lunch, could be dangerous. Similarly, his friend Enzo Crea was a reckless driver, and nearly killed them all when he drove the car off a mountain road into a valley while on a tour of the Abruzzi in 1959 – a near-death experience which haunted Francis for years.

It is notable that much of his time in Italy passed without the neurosis, depression or chronic self-doubt that coloured his daily life in Cambridge; the only occasions when anxiety is mentioned are when he is waiting for letters from home, triggering his worries that his friends have forgotten him or no longer like him: 'eaten up with self-pity because of no letters from Cambridge. What does friendship mean? Why, why, do I have to be so dependent on others?' (3 March 1952). Going back to England, as he did in the autumn of 1953, brought back all of those concerns more intensely than ever before.

# 7

# Larissa and the Biennale, 1962

*The Biennale – Chosen as Commissar – Losing the Exhibits –*
*Strangled Rats – Learning Italian – Free Dinners –*
*Travels around Italy – Lord Snowdon*

Larissa was chosen to head the Soviet contribution to the 1962 Venice Biennale by Nikita Khrushchev personally; not because of her suitability, but because of her age. It was – and in some ways still is – the most prestigious modern art show in the world, and after a decade and a half of peace it was finally getting back onto its feet. The Biennale dates back to 1895, and began as an exhibition of art to celebrate the silver wedding of the then King of Italy, Umberto I. Over the years it expanded into a biannual event, accepting entries from foreigners – which began to be exhibited in national pavilions in 1908 – with the express aim of bringing together 'the most noble activities of the modern spirit without distinction of country'. This was tempered by the way it acted as an art market for exhibitors, but it was still very much part of the optimistic internationalism which also produced the Olympics in 1896 and which dramatically hit the buffers in August 1914.

Russia began to come just as the war was starting, and the next two were cancelled, but from 1920 onwards the new Soviet Union used the event to show off the glories of Soviet art until the next war shut the art world down again.

Foreign currency was a perennial problem for the Soviet government, and it could not afford to waste it. Certainly, the government disliked people dying while abroad, and in late 1961 a 70-year-old curator organising an exhibition died in Sweden. Getting him back cost a fortune:

> Khrushchev personally signed all the big foreign currency payments for the Ministry of Culture. They brought him the bill for a zinc coffin to bring back the body. It was a huge sum of money. The second was for Guber to go to the Biennale and Khrushchev saw that he was 60, and he said, 'Do you have anyone younger?'

Andrei Guber was an art critic, an old stager who produced articles along the lines of 'Abstractionism Is the Enemy of Truth and Beauty' and who had denounced the 1958 Biennale for the 'futility of its reactionary trend'. He was in all respects perfect for the job except for his age: at least he knew something about modern art, even if he didn't like it. Larissa, in contrast, knew nothing at all. But she was young and clean – military family, no relatives abroad. According to Larissa, after deciding Guber was too old, Khrushchev picked up a pile of profiles, came across her application for a grant to go to Paris and said, 'She looks healthy. Send her.'

The episode further illustrates the extent to which the after-effects of the war turned this period in the Soviet Union into something of a land of opportunity for educated women. Under normal circumstances there would have been no possibility of a

Larissa, the Hermitage, *c.* 1961

woman as young and inexperienced as Larissa being chosen for
such a prominent role, but she benefited once more from the
carnage of the war. There were simply not enough men left, and
women found that the world opened up as they were brought
in to fill the gaps. For a generation or more, they managed to
win positions of seniority and responsibility unimaginable in the
1930s, and rare in the West until the 1980s. The curator of the
1960 exhibition had also been a woman – the then 38-year-old
Irina Antonova – and Larissa was now another of the beneficiaries.
She had never organised an exhibition, and had only once been
abroad – on a bus tour of Italy with a carefully monitored group
in 1961. Moreover, her knowledge of Italian was limited, and she
knew little about the art she would be promoting.

It didn't matter; she was summoned to the Ministry of Culture to meet a man called Polikarp Lebedev, who considered the Impressionists to represent a stage in the decay of capitalism, and asked if she knew anything about Soviet art?

'No,' I replied, and he said, 'Well you have one week to learn.' I started going to Moscow about every three days. It was a very strange life, getting to know all the painters. And then I was told to prepare an introductory article for the exhibition catalogue. Lebedev asked me: 'What is the main feature of Soviet art?' I said I didn't know. So he told me: 'the main feature of Soviet art is that it truthfully reflects Soviet life.' Then I had to see his deputy, Alexander Khalturin, who also asked if I knew the main feature of Soviet art. I said that I did and I told him. But he said, 'No. You've got it wrong. the main feature of Soviet art is optimism.' So I wrote in the catalogue that Soviet art reflected Soviet life optimistically.[1]

From the beginning, the Biennale specialised in contemporary art, often to the point of causing scandal. Picasso's *Famille de Saltimbanques* was removed in 1910 for fear of causing offence. In the 1950s the US sent works by Willem de Kooning, Jackson Pollock, Georgia O'Keefe, Alexander Calder. Britain sent Henry Moore, Francis Bacon and Lucian Freud. The most acclaimed artists were chosen as national heroes, their works sent to Venice as a means of projecting some particular image – progressive, modern, dynamic – of the countries they represented.

While making the choice varied from country to country, in the Soviet Union it was certainly far too important to be left to someone like Larissa. She was not given any say about which works of art were to be sent – that had already been done before she was appointed – but even so, the theme of the show was radically

Viktor Popkov, *The Builders of Bratsk Hydro-Electric Power Station,*
1960–1

different from anything that had gone before and reflected the temporary thawing of the country post-Stalin.[2] The artists came from a much wider area geographically, and were much younger – the most prominent work being a vast painting by the 30-year-old Viktor Popkov.

The exhibition, however, had little to do with Larissa's emphasis on optimism in her introduction. Rather, the new freedom introduced by the passing of Stalin permitted a brief period where more open reflection – particularly on the traumas of the war – could be expressed. The result was what was termed 'severe romanticism' – still paintings of workers and working life, but now tired and thoughtful, far from the happy contributors to the Communist-Paradise-to-Come that populated the art of the 1930s.

The exhibition met with little favour – too traditional for Western Modernists, too modern for Soviet Traditionalists. Francis thought it terrible. Popkov himself fell from grace in the

Soviet Union when the thaw turned to a freeze following the Cuban Missile Crisis; he took to drink and was eventually shot and killed in 1974.[3] After the fall of Khrushchev in 1964, the choice of exhibits for Venice became duller and more conservative.

---

Fronting the Soviet exhibition at the world's most important art show was an important role, but it was not without drawbacks. It potentially opened a way for Larissa to advance in the world of bureaucracy and administration, but at the risk of ruining her reputation within the world of academics and curators, which was the one that was important to her. Her friends at the Hermitage urged her not to go, and to find a way out of it – 'Refuse at once. If you do it you will be despised as an art historian' – but the decision had come from the top, and there was little that could be done. Besides, the possibility of spending time in Venice was far too tempting to resist; most Commissars sent there had no profes-sional interest in the city – Antonova focused on Impressionism and Guber was a critic – but Larissa was now fully engaged with the drawings of Tiepolo and eighteenth-century Venetian art in general. Going to the Biennale offered possibilities of doing her own research which might never come again.

Getting there was harrowing, however. All the paperwork was in place by the middle of May, the catalogue written, the visas delivered. Larissa supervised the loading of the railway wagon with the exhibits and was given her final instructions: under no circumstances should she let the works of art out of her sight until they reached their destination. Within twenty-four hours she'd lost them. This, she maintained, was not her fault; rather, it was the doing of the Ministry of Culture, which was again trying to save foreign currency. She, and the restorer who was sent with her, had normal passenger tickets; the exhibits were sent as commercial freight, which cost less. So, halfway along the journey, the freight wagon was uncoupled and sent off on a slower, longer, cheaper route. Larissa only realised what was happening when she glanced out of the window and saw the Soviet entry to the Venice Biennale disappearing into a late snowstorm, heading towards Austria.

Her own train didn't stop until Prague, where she did the only thing possible: she burst dramatically into tears and hurled herself on the mercy of Czech officialdom. This was a technique which often served her well when she got herself into trouble. In this case, officialdom reacted in a gentlemanly fashion; she was transferred to a faster train to head off in pursuit, and arrived in Vienna only a short while after the exhibits themselves: 'At every station, a man would shout "Where's the young woman who's lost her wagon?"' All was well, or should have been, but Larissa was so entranced by the prospect of being in Vienna that she decided that, as the paintings had done so well on their own, they could fend for themselves a little longer. 'I didn't want to look after that wagon. I just wanted to see the city … it was wonderful.' When she did leave on the final leg to Venice, the exhibits were abandoned again, and only arrived a week later – all present and undamaged.

The cavalier approach to orders that she had inherited from her parents now came into full view, and it is striking that the one time disobeying instructions really got her into trouble was the one occasion when she was not at fault. At all other times over the next two years she bent the rules to breaking point and often beyond, getting away with it every time. In Venice, for example, her Italian visa was granted on the strict condition that she should not leave the city, an instruction that she began to ignore more or less from the moment of her arrival.

She was not sent on her own; there is a photograph of her having lunch in a restaurant with Igor Tarasov, the restorer, and a man from the KGB who came up regularly from the embassy in Rome to check on them. But it was easy to escape them; Tarasov merely wanted to go home as he had no interest in Italy – according to Larissa he had no interest in anything except for the legs of Italian women – and the 'man from the embassy' was soon exhausted and bored by her relentless desire to see churches, museums and paintings. Equally importantly, she was the head of the delegation and the one entrusted with the money, which gave her considerable bargaining power.

Although Tarasov was an expert restorer, he had no feel for the things he was restoring, and the prospect of having to spend months in Italy filled him with despair, as he had assumed he would only be away from home for a week or so. Ordinarily, the Soviet delegation did little more than take the exhibits to Venice, set up the pavilion, attend the opening ceremony, and leave; but in 1962 there was a plan to send the display on to Belgrade when the Biennale closed,

The Russians in Venice, 1962 (*left to right*: Tarasov,
the man from the KGB, Larissa)

and for this reason the powers that be decided the pair should stay throughout, so that they could make the arrangements to move everything from Italy to Yugoslavia in October. Larissa, of course, was delighted and in addition found a way to ensure that Tarasov did most of the work setting up, although a small earthquake, which damaged the West German and Soviet pavilions, meant having to organise structural repairs as well. Larissa managed to fix her pavilion, and lent her clothes iron to Tarasov so he could glue a torn painting back together, but the German building fared less well: 'One of the artists said that the pavilion represented his memories and his memories had been destroyed. So he knocked it down.'

Then there was the grand ceremony to start the exhibition off, followed by a reception at the Soviet pavilion, which Larissa had to organise. She had never done anything like it before, but the Brazilian delegation took pity on her and told her what to do and how to do it.

We had a wonderful opening. The President of Italy came and Italians in their fantastic uniforms came. One of the artists from a South American country was refused permission to exhibit his pictures. These consisted of huge rats which he had painted different colours. So, he stood at the entrance with live rats and released them … A colonel strangled one with his bare hands … I made lots of friends and it was all very successful.

After a few days, all the dignitaries had come and gone – Larissa escorted both Stravinsky and the film director Andrei Tarkovsky around the Soviet show. Then the general public was allowed in, and her duties came to an end. Security was light and handled by the Biennale staff, and she gave the restorer the job of going every day to make sure all was well. For her part,

'I never went. I did whatever I liked ...' She considered herself free to do as she pleased for almost four months, and set about learning Italian first of all, as she had only enough to read books and catalogues. This meant practising on newly acquired Italian friends over dinner and trips to the cinema almost every afternoon. This was a particular pleasure, as Larissa loved the cinema as much as Francis, and was keen to see the latest productions. This was not because post-war Russians had been largely cut off from Western cinema with offerings carefully controlled by the authorities, as one book has suggested:[4] 'We saw them all. The army in Germany stole everything and sent it back in trucks. We saw new American films as quickly as Germans did. Not officially, of course ...' But the building of the Berlin Wall nine months before Larissa arrived in Venice changed that: the illicit flow eastwards was disrupted, and it was beginning to look as though it might never be restored.

Money, though, was a perpetual problem; the Soviet government did not believe in subsidising a life of luxury, and after the accommodation was paid for, the two Russians only had enough for one meal a day, which they normally ate in a cheap restaurant near their very basic *pensione*. Larissa found that friendship was just as valuable as hard currency, however. She was adopted by a wealthy couple of Armenian extraction who were renting a palazzo on the Grand Canal for the summer and liked to listen to Larissa talk in Russian. Then there was Sandro Bettagno, one of the Biennale organisers and the head of the Fondazione Cini, an arts organisation set up in the spectacularly beautiful monastery of San Giorgio by a wealthy businessman.[5] They hit it off immediately, becoming friends for life. Bettagno realised that Larissa could not afford decent food, and for reasons of national pride was reluctant to admit it. So he kept on inviting her to lunch and kept on picking up the bills. With the Brazilians frequently asking her out as well, she ate far better than her restorer, who was occasionally invited along, but was too unsociable to accept. Besides, he didn't like Italian food.

She was in an earthly paradise for someone with her speciality and made good use of the opportunity. The holdings of drawings in Venice itself are enormous, and she visited almost every archive and museum that she could get into. But Venetian painters were successful, and popular; they travelled far and wide to undertake commissions across Italy and beyond, and so Larissa, like Francis before her, set off to follow in their footsteps. She travelled the length and breadth of the country, visiting museums, churches and archives, getting to know collectors, librarians and curators.

She was particularly interested in the villas by Palladio scattered around the north-east of Italy, many of which Venetian artists had decorated. She would turn up and ask to be let in; generally speaking in those simpler days, the owners obliged. One such was the aesthete son of a banker, Albert Clinton Landsberg, who had bought and restored the Villa Malcontenta with some friends. Landsberg, a man 'whose body was covered from head to foot with tattoos of the most exceptional obscenity', only used the villa a few weeks a year, but he was there when Larissa appeared to examine some murals by Giovanni Battista Zelotti.[6] So was Lord Snowdon, Princess Margaret's photographer husband, and the art critic John Russell. Larissa examined her pictures, Snowdon photographed her as she leaned out of a window to do so, and Russell wrote about it in the *Sunday Times* in December, complete with the photograph.

This spooked Larissa, who had no idea that hard evidence of her rule-breaking might be splashed over one of the most widely circulated newspapers in the Western world: she saw it herself at a newsstand in Belgrade and wrote to Francis, whom she had now met, to find out how it had happened: 'I am very curious but still

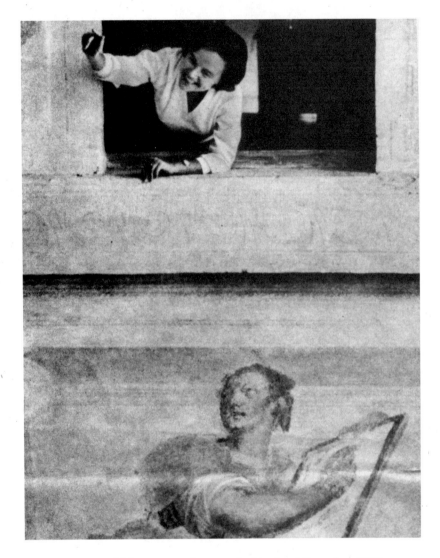

Larissa at Malcontenta, photographed by Lord Snowdon, 1962

frightened …' (LS to FH, 29 December 1962). Even worse, it began to be reprinted in Italian newspapers the following year as well. But if either the Italian authorities or the KGB were annoyed that she should have so brazenly disregarded her instructions, they did not trouble to mention it to her.

# 8

# Francis: London and Cambridge, 1953–1962

*Money Problems – The House of Commons – Homosexuality Debate – Years of Therapy – Friends, Networks and Obligations*

Once he returned from Italy, Francis had a problem: he was nowhere near finishing his book which had expanded beyond a mere thesis on the Jesuits and was now a hugely ambitious study of seventeenth-century Italian art, a project that would take many more years to complete. But he had no income to support such an undertaking; he had used up the limited goodwill of both his parents and his college during his Italian sojourn. He was too junior to apply for an academic position – and could not acquire the experience needed to get one without some occupation that both paid fairly well and demanded little in return.

So in December 1953 he went to work for the House of Commons. Specifically a position as a junior library clerk which a friend had mentioned to him over dinner. 'Qualification – under 26, 1st or 2nd class degree, knowledge of one foreign language.' He wrote a letter and was summoned to an interview: 'It began with a series of questions on Italy and the Baroque.' They asked whether he had any strong political views; he assured them he disliked all politicians equally, and a week later he got a letter offering him the post.[1]

It was ideal: his new employers happily allowed him to postpone starting for a month so he could finish his formal thesis and the job came with three months' holiday a year and an income of £600 – which was quite reasonable as he could live with his parents rent-free. For much of the time, duties were light: 'I spent hours and hours, more or less undiscovered, carrying on with my translations during office hours … and as all the newspapers were there, one tended to read most of them …'

His task was to fact-check statements and provide information to any Member of Parliament who asked, but not all that many did. Few MPs knew that the Research Division where he worked existed, and the two people who comprised it did not rush to advertise their services. But enough got through to give a variety of work: 'the most boring involved, say, looking up references to Committees of Inquiry on drainage in the Isle of Wight.' Sometimes an MP needed more, most interestingly Desmond Donnelly, a Labour MP who managed to combine great enthusiasm for nuclear weapons with a belief that his party was far too right wing.

Donnelly had been pushed into making a short speech to the House on decriminalising homosexuality even though he knew little about the issue and cared less. Francis amassed all the historical background and Donnelly – who was wary of speaking on the subject at all ('I had twins the other day, so no-one can accuse me') – took him to tea to find out what he should say. There was no chance of the law being changed, however: he told Francis that would have to wait until there was a Labour government with a big majority.[2] But Francis provided all the information he needed and gave him the essence of the argument that ultimately ensured success – that is, the King's Cambridge mantra of 'Adult, Private, Consenting' – to fend off attacks on the grounds of moral collapse and the corruption of youth. Francis was quite proud of his effort but was reprimanded by his superiors for trying to influence an MP – his job was to provide facts, not opinions – and he might have been in trouble had he not been about to leave anyway.[3]

In this period he also honed further his skills as an observer of people, using the politicians and his fellow librarians for practice. One colleague, Ian Grimble, became a close friend – 'good-looking and enchanting. Very intelligent, somewhat intolerant perhaps, touchy, quick-tempered, a keen Scotch nationalist.' Another was Roger Morgan: 'lazy, rather a superiority complex … his colleagues mostly disliked him. Yet I liked him … never more so than when I met his wife Harriet: for one feels that anyone who can marry such a wonderful girl must have a lot to him.'[4] And finally there was a young man called Richard Butcher, who made him feel uncomfortable simply by virtue of his background:

lower middle-class, incredibly conscientious and industrious where we were all lazy, he had worked up the hard way. Intelligent but without a spark of 'poetry' … with every prej-udice conceivable, a reader of the *Daily Telegraph*, extremely kind – so much so that one has twinges of guilt even now when criticising him – slow, the 'backbone of England,' – but quite definitely only the backbone.

Seen from a distance of nearly three-quarters of a century, such a portrait seems both snobbish and condescending. Of course it was so, but there were complications in Francis's response. It was not that he disliked or was contemptuous of such people: but he could not find any way of connecting with them – precisely the same problem that he had when he encountered unattached women. His means of communication and emotional contact were so narrowed by his upbringing, his means of getting to know others so particular and literally refined that he simply could not penetrate those whose formation came from outside his circle of experience. In 1954 he reflected on this after dinner with the son of the family he had lodged with when he first came to Rome: 'I was rather shaken to realise that he is ... about my one non-intellectual friend: a friend with whom I have nothing in common. This means that conversation gets a bit difficult ...'

He knew no one who worked outside academia, the arts or the civil service. The working class was an abstract concept – to his credit he did not worship that abstraction as did many of his equally privileged colleagues who were Marxists – and his rare encounters astonished and sometimes appalled him. At Cambridge he found the conversation of the woman who cleaned his rooms so curious he jotted down notes of what she said, rather as an anthropologist might record the sayings of a strange and unknown tribal people. And his encounters with his fellow countrymen while in the army he found so traumatising that at one point he thought being shot at might be preferable.

This made him narrow in reality, but not in the abstract; he genuinely preferred Labour MPs to Conservative ones, even if he had little in common with them and no chance of ever becoming close to them: 'there are few things nastier than ... polished, smooth Tory MPs shouting down a Labour member'. This had no political or ideological component at all; it was again purely personal. He knew perfectly well the impact of the way Labour members were taunted: 'the Tory MPs still look as if they are permanently on top, have never been crushed – like some of those dreadful bullies at Eton ... I felt it powerfully even when I was, so to speak, on their side against the Labour man.'

This last sentence more or less sums up his entire life. The unshakable feeling that he was an outsider in his own milieu was what drove him abroad so frequently: in both Italy and France he could get to know, like, be comfortable with, many of the sort of people he was unable to connect with at home. In England the unspoken signals – dress, accent, manner, bearing – as much as conversational style and content, were too powerful to be overcome, no matter how much he was aware of his limitations, and how hard he tried – on occasion – to set them aside.

The House of Commons was hardly an intellectual wasteland, but nonetheless Francis was relieved to go back to Cambridge in the autumn of 1954. The search for an academic job had borne fruit; he had been given a college fellowship back at King's to teach undergraduates and this provided just enough money to live on. True to form, though, the first thing he did when he left the House of Commons in May was head for Italy, where he stayed for the next four months. The next year he did the same: staying in Cambridge only for as long as the terms lasted and then leaving immediately. The pattern was then firmly established – Holland and Italy in 1956; Germany, Italy and France in 1957; France, Germany and Czechoslovakia in 1958.

This was not through any aversion to his college: King's was the first place where he began to get a true sense of his abilities, and the only institution he ever belonged to that made him feel moderately safe. 'I thought when arriving back here the other night that this is about the only place ... where I can arrive without being frightened ... how wonderful it is to walk through the gates and not feel that I'm going into a prison ...' (24 January 1950). But the price was constant devotion: even married fellows were required to eat in college at least four evenings a week until the 1980s. It was its own world, and brooked few external rivals.

It was perhaps his underlying feeling of exclusion, along with the chronic insomnia which never left him, that led him in May 1956 to begin a course of psychoanalysis that lasted until January 1960. This was his most closely guarded secret, something he scarcely acknowledged even to himself, and he went to remarkable lengths to keep it from others, even though the schedule was punishing – he would leave Cambridge for London on Friday, have an evening session, then another on Saturday. There would be another on Monday and a fourth early on Tuesday morning before he took the train back to Cambridge. He often stayed with the historian Eric Hobsbawm rather than with his parents, lest they begin to ask too many questions. He even left it out of his diaries, only noting appointments in his calendar with an initial. Although the diaries are usually full of passages of self-reflection, one of the few mentions of these sessions came on 1 January 1957, where again even the name of the analyst is hidden: 'By far the most important event of the year for me has been going to L, tho' God knows there's not much to show for it yet. Still, if it works, so many other things may improve.' What he was searching for remains unknown but he found it gruelling: 'Agonising sessions with L' (26 June 1957).

Much of his relationship with Larissa would be determined by learning to trust her in a way he had never managed with anyone else, slowly revealing the secrets that he had continually concealed from others and confronting his fear that he would be rejected. The order in which he did this was curious: a first heart-to-heart in Belgrade involved him nervously confessing his homosexual tendencies. Larissa was unimpressed. Almost pleased, in fact – years later she remarked: 'Of course, Francis was quite homosexual. Until he met *me*.' The second and, as far as he was concerned, the riskier revelation was that he was Jewish, which he did not consciously mention until a few months before they got married. From his vantage point, this made perfect sense: the milieu he came from was largely accepting of homosexuality, but he knew full well – as Larissa learned during the Doctors' Plot as well – that anti-Semitism could erupt unpredictably from the mouths of the most outwardly decent and urbane people. But, once again, Larissa could not have cared less; she had realised it from what he had said on their very first meeting:

so deep was the effect on me of anti-Semitism at Eton, that it needed some steeling of the nerves to tell her that I was a Jew (more, perhaps, than the other confession in Belgrade) … I really couldn't bear her reacting in the wrong way … and then I found that I had told her all this on our very first day together … (1 April 1965)

But he never told her of the therapy. He could have done: when I asked her about it she merely shrugged: 'He never mentioned it. But it doesn't surprise me at all.'

At Cambridge there was a group of like-minded academics who gave him a sense of support and company, although this too was subject to disruption. Periodically, Francis would be reminded of how fragile such friendships were, and how easily they could break down. He saw his world as a bright circle of protection around him, but he was aware of the bleak darkness that lay just beyond: 'all the pub evenings of the last two terms now belong to a remote and happy past, and I sit and brood' (n.d. 1954).

Often enough his sense of security was damaged when someone married, as this did not seem to be a route he would ever follow; his strong friendship with the literary critic Tony Tanner dwindled when Tanner married and his new wife made him choose between her and his friends.[5] Ultimately the arrival of Larissa involved a similar shake-out – his longtime friend, the painter

John Eyles, was always polite to Larissa but was so overcome with jealousy that that friendship ended as well.

Friendship was a variable notion to Francis and can be classed in two distinct groups – close, and what might be termed part of his network. The second is in some ways more instructive, and was vast. Networking is one of the central concepts of the current age, a blend of work, social life and technology, where physical meetings merge with social media to advance careers, win business, or gain renown. But there is nothing new about it except for the style and the fact that it has been democratised: the possibility of networking is now available to all with a phone. Moreover, it is much more obvious, and began to become so when the journalist Anthony Sampson published his *Anatomy of Britain* in 1962 – essentially a dissection of the patronage networks that made the country function and which appeared just as Francis was finishing his own enquiry into the similar networks of seventeenth-century Italy.

In the 1940s and 1950s what is now known as networking was less apparent but far more potent, not least because it was a possibility for very few, and was needed by fewer still; access was one of the most significant divisions between Francis's world and everybody else. Participants were not even particularly aware of what they were doing; it was a natural part of life, and the supreme example of it was the way in which the Apostles, of which Francis was a member, functioned at Cambridge.

Francis belonged to an intermediate generation which has never received a great deal of attention from historians, sandwiched as it was between the one which fought the war and the baby boomers. Its members witnessed the Second World War, but were too young to be participants. They equally lived right through the social revolution of the sixties, but were heading towards an unsuitable middle age when it began to take off – Francis was 40 in 1968. The second period was as much a trickling down of the values of Francis's own world – especially concerning sex – as it was a genuine revolution, but in most respects his generation was more the last of the *ancien régime* than the harbinger of a new one. This world was documented best by Francis's friend and mentor Noel Annan in his book *Our Age* – virtually a prosopography of the Great and the Good of the period, all of whom Annan knew and many of whom Francis knew as well. The title suggested at one level an account of a particular cohort, but equally hinted at the sense of ownership which that particular segment of society had, and which it was on the verge of losing – the age truly was theirs, and they were the last generation with the self-confidence and influence to think so.[6]

But such possession was not a birthright, and it was possible only because of the spider's web of connections that so fascinated Francis. Eton, Cambridge and family gave him potential access to a wide range of people, but such a network did not sustain itself automatically. Rather, it required constant tending and renewal, with any transactional elements wrapped up thoroughly – and preferably sincerely – in friendship and collegiality. The effort involved was prodigious and often exhausting. Constant invitations to tea, lunch or dinner; equally constant attendance at such entertainments given by others; dutifully going to lectures or writing commentaries; long diversions on train journeys to visit people or deliver a present on behalf of someone else; going to railway stations to greet people as they arrived or merely passed through. Francis even took a detour on the way from his wedding to the reception in order to go to the Baltiskaia Hotel and greet the Australian mother of a friend who had just arrived in Leningrad. He ended up taking Mrs Andrews along to the party as well; she was a great success, 'sat talking about Tolstoy on the balcony', and presented the newlyweds with a boomerang (15 August 1965).

Then there was the constant writing of letters telling people your itinerary; noting and remembering the journeys of others;

buying and sending books others might find useful; and finally a never-ending cascade of thank-you letters sent and received, hundreds of them every year. Most important were letters of introduction, connecting people while simultaneously validating them with a quality-control mark. Helping someone reflected back on the person giving the help: Anthony Blunt was severely criticised for trying to foist the unworthy onto universities merely to get rid of them. Favours given, and favours asked, ultimately came into balance – Francis was more often a beneficiary at the beginning of the 1950s, but a decade later it was he who was writing the letters of introduction for others. It was all hard work: he cultivated the author Rosamond Lehmann for some time, having to prove himself of merit and value before he won his prize: 'She is giving me a letter of introduction to Berenson!' (5 January 1952).[7]

Sometimes the process seemed more like applying for a job than merely going to meet someone. In 1955 Francis's friend Umberto Morra wrote a letter of introduction on his behalf to the Countess Anna-Maria Cicogna – perhaps the richest woman in Italy – and Francis sent it to her 'with a covering letter' (14 November 1955).[8] He was then invited to drinks, and as he came recommended, and appeared to be presentable and a potentially useful addition to a dinner table, she thereafter invited him to her palazzo near the Grand Canal whenever they were both in Venice. But the unspoken element of transaction was always there: at a dinner in 1960 he didn't pull his weight because he talked too much with the English theatre critic Kenneth Tynan and ignored the other guests. Cicogna was angry, and they didn't speak again for two years. The friendship never really recovered, not least because Larissa did not like her at all. But, many years later, Francis was still happy to reciprocate when Cicogna's daughter Marina wrote about a forthcoming trip to the Soviet Union: 'I would really like to have an introduction to some friends of yours … it is so important to have human contacts in a new country ... for it is the human beings that make the country' (Cicogna to FH, 7 April 1967).[9]

If Francis was well connected, it was only because he worked ceaselessly to be so. The contrast here is with his own brother, Stephen, supposedly cleverer than Francis himself and with the same family and education, but who was largely unconcerned with the linkages that his elder sibling needed so desperately. Moreover, it did not come without cost, at least in England. Dinner parties were analysed to see if they went well; and from an early age Francis worried over even minor interactions to see if they had been satisfactory – after walking past Duff Cooper, a fellow Etonian and the British Ambassador in Paris in 1946, he wrote, 'I wonder if he noticed my tie?'

Not surprisingly, such possibilities did not exist for Larissa, whose social world was simultaneously more constrained and broader. Social networks did exist in a very informal, hazy fashion

Anna-Maria Cicogna *c.* 1955

in the Soviet Union, but they did not have the complex structure of the Western European variety. The dominance of the
Communist Party made it the ultimate networking facility both
in the Soviet Union and abroad. It was much more complicated
– and dangerous – to trust others; a mere recommendation from
a friend was nowhere near enough. 'I divided people into two
categories: whether you could put your finger in their mouth or
not ... My mother also knew who she could and couldn't trust.
It's pure instinct and doesn't depend on any rationality.' When
abroad, Larissa was more prone to making errors in judgement,
which got her into trouble, but in Russia her judgement was near
perfect, although it did mean that she had to avoid some people
she would otherwise have liked to have known better: 'Those who
you couldn't trust were usually cultivated and intelligent people
but you had to keep away from them. No matter how silly other
people were, we knew we could trust them.'

Some groupings did exist, although it is unclear how strong was
the old noble connection; if it did have a role of any importance it
has not been very well investigated. But mutual recognition with
Tregubov of this shared background saw Larissa and her mother
through the siege of Leningrad, and later saved Tregubov himself.
Similarly, it seems to have been a factor in the way Larissa was
chosen by Dobroklonsky as his favourite. A network of fellow
Leningraders was useful too, providing accommodation in
Moscow and Ufa, while Vera frequently put up visitors from army
officers to ballet dancers who passed through the city; one dancer
later smuggled a picture out of the country for her when Larissa
left it behind after her marriage. In Italy and in Yugoslavia she
quickly got to know many people in the museum and academic
world, who drove her around the country, fed her, found people
to assist her in purloining paintings and – most importantly –
provided her with a husband.

# 9

# Meeting, 1962

*Francis Finishes a Book and Gains an Income – Operation*
*– In a Bad Mood – Meets a Soviet Commissar –*
*Francis Besotted – Larissa also Besotted – Trieste –*
*Earplugs – Larissa Arrested*

Neither Francis nor Larissa was wealthy. In her case this is not surprising, and Larissa certainly felt rich in comparison to many of those around her – her father was paid well as a colonel in the army, and when he was on active duty his expenses were all covered, so his entire salary went straight to Larissa's mother. When Vera was called up during the latter part of the war to work in a hospital, then it all went to Larissa, which was one of the reasons why she enjoyed that period so much. But pay as an employee of the Hermitage was not great and was adequate only because she did not have to worry about housing. Still, it was hard to make ends meet, and like her mother and most women she took on jobs on the side. Vera was an expert seamstress and made clothes for many of her friends and neighbours; they would provide the material and a photograph, often taken from a Western magazine, and she did the rest. Larissa did watercolour illustrations and proof-reading for books and wrote captions for booklets and postcards. 'I did other things the entire time because I needed money. The publishers paid very well, even if you just wrote titles for the postcards. I was always producing something.'

Francis was in a similar position until 1962, the year in which he not only met Larissa, but also won a coveted university position at Cambridge as librarian of the fine arts faculty – a job which paid £600 a year, the same as the House of Commons, and was added to his college fellowship at King's, which carried a stipend of £350 a year. He did get free accommodation and meals, but his situation was not luxurious, and until then, like Larissa, he had to pick up jobs on the side to make ends meet – lectures for other universities and reviews of books, all of which brought in a further £134 in 1958. His father had been subsidised heavily throughout his life by his own parents, but never felt much desire to give similar support to his own children. But Jacob Silas, perhaps realising that his son was not the most generous of people, had left a sum of money in trust for his three grandchildren, which generated £195 a year each. Before the university job, all these provided him with £680 a year in the late 1950s – pretty much the level of the average working man's wage at the time. By 1963 his position had changed dramatically – the university job also meant more opportunities for teaching, lecturing and translating, he was getting royalties on his first book, and his total income increased to nearly £1,800. This was finally, at the age of 35, an adequate – if not extravagant – income, about the level at which someone as ultimately middle-class and respectable as he might consider marriage to be a practical possibility.[1]

The book – entitled *Patrons and Painters* – was important because of the gigantic boost it gave to his self-confidence and career. It was huge; the initial project he had begun a decade earlier had expanded dramatically as there was little institutional pressure to hurry; apart from reviews, he had only published one proper academic article by the time it appeared. Nevertheless, while he was writing it he lived a sort of professional half-life, regarded as having immense potential but yet to prove himself fully. But he was getting to the end of the period where he could survive on potential, and publication was very much a make-or-break moment. A more secure person would have been nervous; Francis was a wreck in the months before his book finally came out in early June 1963, and these were the very months when he met and became ever more involved with Larissa. As he looked through the final text he wrote, 'I feel like paying the publisher to cancel it' (9 November 1962). During the proof-reading process he had lamented 'the stodginess and cowardice of my book' (2 November), and found that 'The book depresses me more and more' when he thought of its publication (20 November). As he reread it later (the dedication now changed 'to L.S.'), he found that 'whenever I look into it I am again appalled by its flatness, its flabby inelegance ...' (10 January 1963). The first copy, which arrived shortly after his first trip to see Larissa in the Soviet Union, rattled him even more: 'I have already discovered two catastrophic misprints – this has depressed me beyond words, especially as one is in the very first paragraph' (19 May 1963).[2] And at 6.45 on the evening of 23 June he was hanging around the railway station in Turin, waiting for the English Sunday newspapers due on the 7.30 train from Paris and killing time by sitting in a bar and scribbling in his diary: 'There is supposed to be a review of my book by Gombrich.' There was, but he had a long, anxious wait before he could see what the verdict was: the train was late. Only at 9 p.m. did he scribble another note – brief but dripping with relief: 'I've read the review, and it's excellent.'[3]

It was more than that: Ernst Gombrich, who the *New York Times* later said 'may be the most famous art historian of all time' (24 November 1996), and whose opinion Francis greatly valued, had the reputation and authority to make a career. The long, carefully analytic review, which said all the right things (admirable, splendid, scrupulous), and others like it which came in subsequently, moved Francis from the status of virtual graduate student into being one of the most innovative authorities on Italian art. His decade-long gamble had paid off handsomely.

That fortunate denouement had to wait, however: while Larissa went to Venice in 1962 still missing her father, worried about her mother's health, and increasingly detached from her marriage, Francis arrived contemplating the bleak future he could see stretching out in front of him. She found the beauty of Italy profoundly healing, while for him the magic failed to work. Losing the focus of his research project led him to scrutinise the value of what remained in his life, and he didn't like what he saw. Often in this period he shuddered at his possible fate as 'a civilised man-of-the-world old buffer don' (30 October 1962). The theme that had popped up regularly ever since he began his diary was back with a vengeance and an aching, existential and despairing loneliness overcame him:

I feel that the world is divided into the happy and the unhappy, and that happiness only comes from a really close relationship with someone else ... I remember, four years ago, when driving in the Abruzzi with Enzo and Grazia, Sandro and Cincia, how when the crash came their first cries were all for each other, and for a few moments I was left, surrounded by my closest friends, in total solitude. (8 September 1962)

His usual pleasures began to fade: 'with the book finished that sense of purpose which, alas, is so vital to me, has gone out of my visits to Rome'. Even Paris was losing its appeal: 'Though we (Enzo was there) saw lots of charming people, old friends, new ones, I'm feeling bitter and hostile in general and a sort of loathing comes over me ...' (20 March 1962). And there were ever more examples of how fragile his group of friends actually was. One by one, his closest circle was crumbling under the impact of people getting married, taking up jobs in America, or getting divorced: 'Oh God! Oh God! The end of an epoch that meant such a lot! ... What a hellish time this has been for good-byes' (10 August 1962).

In addition, he had had an operation – never specified what for, but evidently digestive – so he cancelled a holiday in Hungary and instead went off to stay with his friend Umberto Morra and recuperate in the garden of his villa near Cortona. He was in a bad mood, finding little solace in the people he met, and in addition still feeling enfeebled. Then to Venice, but even it failed to dent

Francis in Venice, 1962

his implacable misery. He made up with Anna-Maria Cicogna after two years' silence, but now saw her in a new, and more critical, light as a woman with 'all the "right" opinions ... brusquely arrogant, ready to switch off interest at any moment' (26 August 1962). He stopped off at the Piazza San Marco, which had always entranced him but which he now found to be only 'Venice at its tamest, safest, most easily digestible' (29 August). He went to the Accademia, 'hardly looking at anything'; to an exhibition of past prizewinners of the Biennale, and concluded that every year was worse than its predecessors; and to the Biennale itself, which he found dreadful and boring.

In this unshakably black mood he went to see his old friend Sandro Bettagno, who tried to cheer him up by offering him a spare ticket for a concert at the Fondazione Cini. Bettagno also asked him if he wanted to meet a Soviet Commissar, one 'L. Salmina from Leningrad', to whom he had given the other spare ticket. Francis had no desire at all to meet such a person, but wanted the distraction and liked being with Sandro, and so he accepted.

As it turned out, the music was 'pleasant, but no more', and Bettagno went home soon after it finished. For Francis,

> the real discovery was Salmina, with whom I sat chatting till about 1:30 ... She is rather pretty and immensely attractive with, as so often in Russians, absolutely no poise whatsoever so that one is often surprised by the clumsiness of her stance or movements. She is wholly delightful, full of enthusiasm, gay, always bursting into laughter, exceedingly intelligent and cultivated. I could marry someone like her – she is already married to an ex-naval officer of 35, 'much older' than she is, as she pointed out. (29 August 1962)

Mentioning her lack of poise was a touch of the old and defensive Francis, but at least it was exactly what Larissa's own father had also said when he saw what the famine and siege had done to her eating habits – 'Dear God, I hope you never go abroad; your table manners are a disgrace to Russia.' Besides, rarely for Francis on the subject of women, it was the only vaguely critical remark he ever made about her.

He had often in the past said that he could marry someone he had met, but that was always when he knew he was never going to see them again, when they were manifestly uninterested in him, when they were already married or, on one occasion, when he met a woman who had been diagnosed with a terminal disease and only had a few months to live. Certainly, he knew of this tendency. Writing of a Portuguese woman he met in Paris in 1955, he said: 'Why do I always meet wonderful girls when there is no chance of seeing them again? Or is it just because of this that I decide they are wonderful?' (16 April 1955). It is more than likely that this time he was open to Larissa simply because he assumed she was unavailable – and as a Soviet Commissar with a husband in Russia and a KGB minder nearby, she certainly should have been. Consequently, he felt completely unthreatened: 'we discussed films, ballet (including Nureyev) literature, music, art etc. etc.[4] I took to her enormously, and felt completely relaxed' (29 August 1962).

Larissa was surprised at the consequences of this – 'I liked him enormously but he started to appear uninvited at my hotel ...' Still, she accepted a second invitation, which Francis again recorded in detail:

We then went to dinner at the Malamocco and ... talked of everything with no inhibitions.[5] She is deeply patriotic; says that she has never felt the lack of intellectual Liberty in

Russia; that she imagines that no people in the world are as
self-critical as the younger generation of Russians. And of this
younger generation she gave a wonderful (and convincing)
picture: alert, cultivated, warm and intelligent ... I found her
so attractive, buoyant and brave and receptive, full of jokes
yet sensitive and 'Russian' ... (4 September 1962)

The feeling was rapidly becoming mutual. When Francis
mentioned he was going to Trieste to visit friends, she felt such a
sense of panic that she decided she had fallen in love.

Francis, in contrast, simply did not understand what his own,
similar feelings were. He found himself thinking of her all the
time, looked forward to seeing her with an unusual sense of anticipation, but had no idea what it meant. However, it did not occur
to him that he might cancel his forthcoming trip to Trieste, and
he was very surprised when Larissa told him she would come and
join him. For her, this was a serious step, complicated still further
as she was still not meant to leave Venice and also had scheduled
a meeting at 10 a.m. the day after to go over the accounts with the
'man from the embassy'.

While she was worrying whether she dare take the risk, Francis
was enjoying one of those evenings in male company which he
found so rewarding:

a Slav restaurant, high above Trieste, where we ate excellent
fish. Then the evening turned into ... a story about Italy.
At an adjoining table to ours, two fat, elderly men began
singing extracts from opera, folk songs, etc., with rich trem-
olo and all the mannerisms of great operatic performers (but
scarcely the voice). They were soon joined by everyone in the
restaurant – a characteristically *piccolo borghese* public. Nino
got out a guitar, he and Enzo began singing and for about

an hour the whole room echoed with music and drink and happiness …[6] I have rarely spent a more moving evening … (4 September 1962)

But the next morning, Larissa arrived, and he got to spend an entire day of the sort that he had never thought possible. They walked around the city and discussed the buildings, went to the museum and talked about the paintings; he sat nearby as she took notes on the Tiepolos in the prints and drawings department. Then they went for a relaxed dinner as a couple with his friends and, at the end, Larissa announced that she had missed the last train back, and what was she going to do?

They decided that she would have to get a room at Francis's hotel, and in the morning Enzo Crea would drive them both back to Venice – a nearly three-hour drive, so they would have to leave early. The dinner broke up, and she walked with Francis to the hotel. He complained the whole way about how the street noise kept him awake all night: 'I asked if he had any earplugs and he said he did but he couldn't put them in. I said I could do it for him. I was absolutely sure that this was a pretext for him to come to my room …'

It wasn't. He turned up shortly afterwards in his pyjamas, with a large earplug in either hand. Larissa decided that it was time to take charge of the situation.

———————

The next morning, they drove back to Venice and Larissa arrived just in time for her meeting. After the initial encounter, however, there was nothing to suggest that the relationship was likely to develop further. Neither changed their plans, and while they exchanged letters, it would have been perfectly straightforward for the whole episode to become merely 'the stuff of a future memory, rather than of actuality' (31 December 1962).

But they wanted to meet again; Francis went to Rome but then came back to Venice to see her. When he said he wanted to go to Bologna for an exhibition on landscape painting by Poussin and Claude,[7] the temptation was too great to resist, and Larissa went along as well even though it meant violating the terms of her visa yet again. This time she wasn't so lucky. They stayed overnight, and the following day Francis took her to see the Byzantine mosaics of Ravenna. 'We had booked into a hotel and, when we were coming back from Ravenna, there was a man sitting outside. He said, "Larissa Salmina, I have come here to see you." He said I was being arrested ...'

By Francis's account, it was at least a politely Italian business:

He was rather sympathetic and embarrassed and hated having to do the job but insisted ... the hotel spying system had obviously worked efficiently, for when I went up to talk to him he said at once 'Lei è il critico d'arte che è venuto qui per la mostra.' [You are the art critic who came here for the show.] He asked me how I had enjoyed the exhibition, and told me to console Larissa who was now crying. This crying probably saved the situation, for he turned a blind eye when we proposed leaving for Venice only the next morning. (29 September 1962)

It was worrying nonetheless, and Larissa was alarmed they might lodge a protest with the Soviet Embassy. But even this did not make them rush: instead of hurrying back to report at the Venice Questura the next morning as promised, they decided to go to the exhibition again, then had a long lunch, and returned so late that the Questura had closed for the weekend. So they left again and went to the Hotel Cipriani on the island of Torcello for a night that Francis decided 'marked the climax of my life so far'.[8] So much so that they stayed on the next day, had 'a superb lunch' and only slowly took the vaporetto back in the afternoon to Venice 'and the world of questuras'.

Even though they were two days late by that stage, it was all sorted out quickly enough. Larissa apologised, the police explained the rules as if she didn't know them full well already, and reassured her they would not take the matter any further. The moment she had finished promising to be good in future, she went straight to the railway station to catch a train with Francis to Milan. She stayed there overnight, spent the day with him until he caught the train back to England, and returned to Venice and legality late that evening. The pattern for the next three years was already set.

How did all this happen? It is perhaps a good idea to pause here, because the business of falling in love is such an impenetrable phenomenon – nearly everyone does it at least once, but it takes many forms and, despite many thousands of years of investigation by everyone from poets to neurologists, it remains the greatest mystery of human existence. Who? Why then? Why there? None of these are ever easy to answer convincingly. Even stranger is the way that it happens, and the strangest of all is the thunderbolt, *coup de foudre* in French, *colpo di fulmine* in Italian – nearly all languages have a similar phrase for it – that sudden near instantaneous certainty that the person you just met is the love of your life. Plato wrote that souls were divided in two and spent their human lives wandering the earth looking for their other half. It is as convincing as any other explanation that has been put forward.

Francis was aware of many of the reasons for himself – although he never made the connection with finishing his book or his depressed mood of the previous few months. Had he ever bothered to reread his own diary properly he might have been a little clearer. In a sense he had been working towards this moment all his life; he had been infatuated with girls, but they had not been interested in him. He had rejected others even though – perhaps because – they were attracted to him. He had satisfying and close friendships with men – the 'romantic friendships' he complained were now tarnished by Freudian modernity – and some with women, but never came close to merging that with a physical attraction. That side of relationships was always pushed aside and forgotten as quickly as possible. After a short while he could not even remember the name of Dora Holzhandler, the young painter he was attached to in London when he was 21; following a brief relationship with his friend Meriel Stocker in Italy, he never mentioned her name again in his diaries.[9] He did, undoubtedly, have a few homosexual relationships, but these were stripped of any importance, to the point that they are only infrequently and elliptically mentioned, the men involved having no real presence, allowed no personality and not even a name – referred to only by an initial, 'G.' or 'E.' He did not want the unequal companionate marriage of the sort common among his friends in England. He could not abide the Italian approach he first encountered fully in a Roman brothel, with women either idealised on a pedestal or despised in the gutter.

As far as he was concerned, his search was hopeless, but Larissa swept the years of anguish aside in a couple of meetings. He was physically attracted to her, he loved to talk to her, he loved to do and see things with her. He felt comfortable and close at the same time, which was a combination he had never experienced, and had abandoned as a practical possibility.

But that was only half of the problem: he knew – more or less – why he had fallen in love with her; he had no idea why she had fallen in love with him:

It sounds rhetorical anti-rhetoric to say that I don't understand how anyone can possibly fall in love with me: yet this
is the literal truth. Friendship, deep affection yes – I think
I have this gift: but to inspire love, when there are so many
other more attractive people in every way than myself – this
to me has always seemed inconceivable. (4 September 1962)

It is true that, in the months after they met, he did his very
best to persuade himself that he was not in love with her, and as
a last-ditch attempt in 1964 he even took a close friend, the art
historian Benedict Nicolson, to Leningrad to meet Larissa just in
case falling in love with her might be a sign of incipient insanity.[10]
Nicolson thought she was wonderful, though, and gave him a
clean bill of health. Ultimately the evidence overwhelmed even his
defences in the way he missed her, waited for her letters, longed
to see her once more.

So he got no easy answer to that basic question, and Larissa
certainly did not help. She did not seem to think it mattered, and
had no interest in the forensic self-examination that so concerned
Francis. As far as she was concerned, the fact of it was so powerful
that the cause was irrelevant. Mutual interests, similar concerns,
were all important, of course, but such details answer nothing:
many others she had met in her life also met these basic criteria.
I did ask on several occasions, to get just a little more out of her,
but she always either changed the subject or simply shrugged.
The question so central to Francis was one which had no answer
and didn't even deserve one. 'Why? I just did.'

Only one remark gives some sort of hint, and this came when
she was talking about coming to England: 'I wasn't at all sure that
Francis wouldn't leave me, but at least for a short time I would
be happy.' After her history, of the siege, the near starvation, the
constant moving, the purges and the pogroms, she had learned

not to dream of an ideal future which might never come. Such a preoccupation could only taint the present, and she knew that any future at all could be snatched away with little or no warning. Instead, she had learned to grab happiness when it presented itself. If it had to be paid for in due course, then at least she could say she had known it for a while. For Francis, 'extreme self-consciousness is an essential prelude to living' (20 January 1963). For Larissa it was the opposite of living.

# 10

# Encounters, 1963–1965

*Trouble with a Matisse – Letters – Meetings in Leningrad*
*and Paris – Francis in a Panic – Guy Burgess's Birthday Party*
*– A Dinner in London – Venice Again –*
*A Disastrous Exhibition*

After their initial time together, the relationship developed its
own logic that swept both of them along almost against their will,
establishing an underlying rhythm which began to take over their
lives. Planning ways of meeting again; waiting for phone calls;
coming back home hoping to see a letter waiting; the disappointment when none had arrived; the exaltation when two arrived
simultaneously; reading them repeatedly, scrutinising envelopes
to see if they had been opened, or if there was any explanation
for why they had taken so long. The occasional silences which
made Francis worry that Larissa was in trouble, or no longer loved
him. All of these moments gave a thrill, a roller-coaster ride of
emotions that was plainly addictive, and a hidden life which was
far more exciting than mundane reality. Both kept their secret
close: in Larissa's case for obvious reasons, and in Francis's because

he was afraid of the humiliation if it didn't work out. He unburdened himself initially only to his friends in Italy and to his father confessors in England – Noel Annan, Dadie Rylands, E. M. Forster, although this last with caution: 'I was reluctant to do this at first because he so hates women – but he was wonderfully kind and affectionate …' (4 October 1962).[1] Francis did not fully trust anybody else, and only began to tell a few English friends of his own age shortly before he went to Leningrad the following year.

Larissa went on more illicit tours of Italy to fill in the time before she left: on 14 September she was in Padua, then to Vicenza, then down to Rome. But she did not stay long, and immediately went on to Milan, Bergamo and Turin, then to Verona and Florence, before finally leaving on 10 October. She was in a hurry to see as much as she could because the Biennale was winding down and the transfer of the entire Russian exhibition to Belgrade had to be organised. She tried to get out of this last stage: Yugoslavia held no particular attraction for her – 'it is not interesting at all and even on the first day was rather dull …' (LS to FH, 20 October 1962). She was desperately homesick for Leningrad and wanted to get back to her mother who was both grieving for the death of her husband and suffering from an assortment of illnesses. She pleaded to be allowed to arrange the exhibition then get on the train home. This was refused, and she ended up having to stay for three months.

It was a mark of Larissa's success in Venice that she was entrusted with this second task, however unwanted, but an event as she was packing up undercut any credit she might have gained in Moscow. Her formidable predecessor as Commissar in 1960, Irina Antonova, had been made director of the Moscow Pushkin Museum the following year. She had wanted to go to Venice again, or at least had wanted to decide who did go. Towards the end of the Biennale, her lover, an art critic called Boris Veimarn, turned up in Venice.[2] Larissa was enchanted by him – 'a real gentleman, so interesting' – and she tried to take him round all the sights. As he was about to leave, he gave her a letter, which instructed her to return to the Soviet Union with a Matisse, *View from a Window in Tangier* (1912), a painting from the Pushkin which had been loaned for the exhibition of previous Biennale winners at the Ca' Pesaro (Matisse had won the Grand Prize in 1950). Veimarn explained that it was a straightforward task, but that he had no time to see to the matter himself.

When all of her own exhibits were packed, Larissa went along to the Italian authorities so that the Matisse could be sent in the same shipment. There she was told that it could not be done: when the painting arrived in Italy, the Pushkin had not declared it, nor filled in any of the necessary forms. As there was no record of it being brought into the country, it was impossible to provide the necessary papers to take it out again. So the picture would have to stay in Italy and might well be confiscated. 'Our painting of Matisse has become now a "National Treasure" of Italy!' (LS to FH, 19 October 1962). One sympathetic official did offer to give her a document stating that the painting was worth less than a million lire – about £500 – which was below the level that required an export licence. But they agreed that even the stupidest of customs officials was unlikely to think that an original oil painting by Matisse would be worth so little – although on the only occasion one did ask questions, it turned out that he had never heard of Matisse.

She was in a bind – under instructions to take the painting home, unable to do so, and equally unable to put the blame on Antonova for having created the mess in the first place, or on Antonova's lover for giving impossible instructions. 'I can't part without it ... better to take it than to sit here who knows how much time.' She also had contradictory orders – both to accompany the Matisse back to Russia and to stay in Belgrade with the Biennale exhibits. She began to suspect that the whole business was a deliberate plan to ruin her career; Antonova was a woman who knew how to bear a grudge and was adept at the game of ensuring others took the blame when things went wrong. There was also an institutional angle: Antonova was from the Pushkin

Henri Matisse, *View from a Window in Tangier*, c. 1912

Museum in Moscow, Larissa from the Hermitage in Leningrad, and each institution thought it should be the dominant force in the Soviet museum system.

As there seemed no better solution, and the wrath of Italy was likely to be less severe than the fury of Russia, Larissa decided simply to take the Matisse. She and Tarasov packed it up – it was quite large, at 115 by 80 centimetres – carried it to the station, and stored it in the toilet of the Belgrade train. The two Russians then took their seats, looking innocent and bewildered when a guard came along calling out, 'Whose is that box in the toilet?'

But there was no customs inspection, and Larissa relaxed: the train was meant to go straight from Venice to Belgrade without stopping, and once over the border they would be safe. 'I told you already I was very stupid.' Unfortunately, it was not a very reliable train: it broke down and limped into the station at the frontier, where they were told to change to a new one on a different platform. And it was then that the customs officials began to do their work. Larissa and her restorer hid until the whistle went to indicate the new train was about to leave, then grabbed the Matisse out of the toilet and ran for it, barrelling down the platform with customs men shouting at them to stop. The restorer jumped on, dragging the Matisse with him, and Larissa leapt on afterwards. The train then trundled through the last few metres of Italian territory until it was over the border, and they were safe.[3]

At Belgrade, they carried the crate to the Soviet Embassy and dumped it in the entrance lobby while Larissa insisted on making a phone call to Moscow; the embassy staff were instructed to take charge of the painting and send it back home. All would have been well, except that the Italian newspapers got hold of the story. 'The press exploded. Huge articles. I was a villain ...' The publicity earned her the undying enmity of Irina Antonova, who took no prisoners. 'She hated me.' Antonova became the longest serving museum director in Russian history and was only removed from her position in 2013 when, at the age of 91, she picked a fight in public with Vladimir Putin because she wanted to transfer Hermitage paintings from St Petersburg to Moscow. She lost. As Larissa said – with a slight smile of satisfaction – whatever else he might be, Vladimir Putin was a good Leningrad boy at heart.

―――――――――

Of necessity, much of Larissa's and Francis's early relationship was written. Their letters were frequently self-censored, and so they discovered much of each other through books, and a discussion of books. It is hard now to grasp the importance of reading to the generation to which both Larissa and Francis belonged. Books were their livelihood and main entertainment, a means of communication, identification and their route to self-understanding. Both read prodigiously; Francis was in many ways the Last Victorian in the massive amount of time he spent reading and digesting what he had read. Like his predecessors, and unlike his successors, he did not have to waste time on practicalities: no trips to the supermarket, dealing with children, commuting to work, cooking or housework. His life was clear to read, and his persistent chronic insomnia meant that he had more time than most to fill in.

Larissa was the same, although her unusual early life meant that she had no opportunity (or perhaps inclination) to leave much of a paper trail. Moreover, she was rather broader in her tastes, developing an abiding passion for detective stories and thrillers of all kinds, especially those from the late Soviet period. But she particularly adored French novels, especially by Dumas, which she read, in French, at an early age: 'I was like the Russian hero at the beginning of the nineteenth century who said that my body was born and lived in Russia, but my heart belonged to the crown of France. For me, Dumas and Paris were where I actually was. England, not so much.'

So, shortly after they met, Francis began to read his way through Turgenev and Fyodor Sologub and reread his Dostoevsky; Larissa meanwhile started on novels by his friends – Forster's *Room with a View* and *Howard's End, Dusty Answer* by Rosamond Lehmann and *The Bell* by Iris Murdoch. She also tackled D. H. Lawrence, read all the English books in her mother's flat, and then started on the type of Italian novel Francis might read as well. On top of that there was their mutual interest in cinema, ballet and music – English music was hardly mainstream in the Soviet Union, but in 1964 Larissa went to see performances of Benjamin Britten's operas which had been brought over for a tour. She liked *Albert Herring*, but was more impressed by *The Turn of the Screw*.[4] 'The music and the whole performance were divine, it made us all paralysed with terror, my mother couldn't sleep at night after it' (LS to FH, 1 November 1964).

Synchronising their tastes and knowledge in such a way was of course a slow business, and their problem was that the world suddenly began to change rapidly following their first dinner together in Venice. The relative Soviet openness to the West – during which Larissa had her first trip to Italy as a student and was able to apply for a scholarship to travel to Paris, then be trusted to go to the Biennale – suddenly began to close. The starting point was the Cuban Missile Crisis, which erupted seven weeks after they met and while Larissa was still in Belgrade. She was not particularly interested: in her surviving letters of the period, it is only mentioned once – 'Everybody is excited about Cuba' (LS to FH, 23 October 1962) – and she was much more alarmed at the prospect of having to stay in Yugoslavia until January. Later she insisted that she was never worried and knew full well that it was all bluster on both sides. Francis, as ever, was far more concerned, although this was largely because the English public was told more about what was going on. For the first time since Korea, his response to the news was personal: 'listened to the news. Leave stopped for Russian army, etc Had a real moment of panic and the dread of a *solitary* death. Longed, more perhaps than ever before, for Larissa to be in my arms again' (24 October 1962).

Larissa was right about the outcome, but wrong not to worry: the near catastrophe of Cuba set the tectonic plates of Russian politics moving. The perception of defeat, when Khrushchev agreed to pull Soviet missiles off the island, weakened his position and made him an easier target for his younger, more hardline rivals. One of the first areas to be hit was art – five weeks after the end of the crisis, Khrushchev delivered a speech denouncing modern art as 'filth, decadence and sexual deviations'. He was eventually toppled two years later, in October 1964, after months of manoeuvring; his successor, Leonid Brezhnev, intensified the internal repression of dissidents and began to reverse the openness to the West. Bit by bit, interactions between the opposing sides of the Cold War became more problematic, which meant that Larissa and Francis had only a limited amount of time to make up their minds what to do with each other.

Francis travelled to see Larissa whenever an opportunity offered. He went to Belgrade in December 1962 for a week, to Leningrad in April 1963, to Venice in October, Paris in November, Leningrad again in April 1964, and twice in 1965, in addition to his other voyages to the USA, Canada, Holland, Italy, France and Spain. Larissa also travelled as much as possible in her own sphere, lecturing in Moscow, Warsaw and Tashkent, as well as taking holidays in East Germany, Latvia, the Caucasus, Crimea and Bukhara (in what is now Uzbekistan). Above all, though, she managed to win permission for another stay in Venice.

At other times, letters had to do, but even these were constrained by the ever-present fear that the Soviet authorities would intercept and read what they wrote. Telephoning was possible, but again there was a chance of wiretaps. The phone system in any case was far from perfect. It was not simply a question of picking up a phone and dialling a number. Neither the Soviet Union nor Britain was awash with phones; Larissa had access to one in her home but was wary of using it to place calls abroad. Francis had one in his rooms at King's, but nonetheless spent a great deal of time hanging around at the Post Office making calls in case listeners in Leningrad spotted a pattern. International calls were expensive and had to be booked in advance, which meant ensuring that the other person knew to be in place. Often enough a success-ful call would mean sending a telegram a few days before, to make sure the other would be there: Larissa once wrote: 'Yesterday I was so excited because I had a hope of hearing your voice ... I telephoned, and spoke to your "portier" ... Oh darling, what a dreadful disappointment, I was ready to cry ...' (LS to FH, 28 October 1962). Even when all went well, the results could be infu-riating: dropped lines, or a connection so bad it was impossible to hear what the other person was saying.

Both of them now had to take the outside world seriously, in Francis's case for almost the first time in his life. Until then, he had had the typical upper-middle-class English disdain for bureau-cracy, be that in England or abroad. Officialdom was annoying, often involved long waits or lengthy forms, but it was not some-thing to fear. He was instinctively confident that it would all get out of his way eventually. World events – he particularly enjoyed the deaths of great figures like George VI in 1952, Stalin in 1953 or Churchill in 1965 – were spectator sports, not matters that could ever concern him personally. Larissa had developed her own way of coping with officialdom and keeping out of trouble, for the most part by simply ignoring everything outside her own world of work and friends as much as possible, or by a strategic display of feminine tears in an emergency. Now they were both coming to the position where neither of their strategies was going to work: if they decided to continue the relationship, and even more if they decided to get married, they would have to take the sort of risks that she avoided, and which terrified him.

Francis kept all of her letters to him during this period, but Larissa, out of a natural sense of caution, destroyed all he wrote to her in Russia until the proposed marriage became known to the authorities there and concealment served no further purpose. She preserved those she received while she was in Italy in 1963, however, leaving them with others and recovering them when she left Russia permanently. When it was safe to do so, both would write to the other at least once a day, sometimes more often.

Letters could be as frustrating as phone calls: even if sent express they were often delayed, or went missing altogether. The Italian post in particular was notoriously erratic and every time a week passed with no word, Francis would worry: 'I still haven't heard a word from you. I do hope that this is just the fault of the Italian Post Office, and that it doesn't mean that something has gone wrong ...' (FH to LS, 13 October 1963). 'I have now had two letters from you, and this has made me much happier' (FH to LS, 16 October). 'Two more of your letters have just arrived this morning – calming me down when I was beginning to get very "agitato"' (FH to LS, 22 October). 'No letter from you, and no prospect of any now until Monday' (FH to LS, 26 October). 'Every day I go for post but useless ... I long so much to hear your news' (LS to FH, 28 October).

They were almost the last generation which relied on letters in this way, and so the last to experience the heady mix of emotions involved in an epistolary romance. For more than two millennia the only means of communication at a distance was through letters, and this produced some of the greatest works of world literature. Francis wrote multiple letters almost every day of his adult life, and there remained in the basement of his house packing case after packing case filled with others received in reply. Larissa's study was also littered with boxes of them. This unique combination of literature, sociability and emotion has now gone; Francis lived just long enough to see the dawn of the new digital age and didn't like it one bit; Larissa could never be bothered with it.

They wrote in two styles depending on where Larissa was. Outside Russia, both could say whatever they wanted as there was little chance of their letters being opened and read; even when in Yugoslavia, Larissa felt confident that she was not going to have her letters intercepted. Also, whenever a Western friend or colleague passed through the Hermitage, a message could be smuggled in and out in relative safety, although even this could occasionally strain the nerves:

I went to see Carla Barbantini who has just returned from Russia having taken a note of mine to Larissa. She told me that at the frontier, she alone ... had been systematically searched, her luggage and papers systematically gone through until my letter – in an unaddressed but closed envelope – was found. The Russian guards ... closely questioned her about the contents of this, eventually forcing her to say to whom it was addressed ... The whole thing makes me rather sick with worry, tho' Carla tells me that Larissa was 'serena, tranquillissima ...' (28 August 1964)

So Larissa's letters from Belgrade begin, 'My dearest darling Francis, it is late in the night and only two days since we were separated ...' (LS to FH, 29 December 1962), and from Leningrad, 'Dear Mr Haskell, I am so sorry for the delay ...' (LS to FH, 6 May 1963).

Francis did not truly possess the spirit of adventure. It is true that he went to live in France and Italy and travelled widely across Europe more generally, but he rarely stepped out of the milieu in which he felt safe. Now he had to venture into the fearful unknown, both because of Soviet officialdom, and because of the ever-growing but unique emotional entanglement with Larissa. But this mixture of elation and disappointment dragged him into a genuine commitment which might not have occurred had everything been easier and more straightforward. The hidden world they created together sustained both of them. Their relationship developed as an intoxicating brew of love story and espionage novel, complete with secret codes, clandestine meetings, smuggled messages, and all the techniques of the spy: '"Giovanni Bellini" was our future marriage. "Tiepolo's son" was our future son. Whenever I told him that a Tiepolo didn't sell, it meant that I wasn't pregnant.' The trouble was that sometimes she really was talking about Tiepolo, which confused Francis no end.

Larissa at least was used to subterfuge. Francis most certainly was not; there was nothing in his character to make him relish any of it. And yet he persisted, travelling on the aircraft he loathed, staying in hotels he detested, and going to countries he feared, simply to keep up the connection with her. Often enough he did not understand why he was doing any of this. But the shared secret was as seductive as it was vital, for Larissa because of the potential consequences for her career and freedom, for Francis because he was afraid of the depression and despair that would seize him if the whole enterprise collapsed. Very swiftly, Larissa became the focal point of his world, giving him life and purpose and more than filling the gaping hole left by his book.

So when he returned to Cambridge for the start of the new academic year, he found that his universe had been turned inside out. He couldn't concentrate very well on his teaching, he began to avoid friends rather than seeking out their company, but he noticed that he was sleeping better, his psychosomatic illnesses were leaving him alone, and his mood, so dark during the summer, had lightened dramatically except when he thought of his life in England. These thoughts generated 'the feeling that real life is escaping me, is going on elsewhere ... real life is emotional life, and all those with whom I feel most emotionally involved are far, far away' (30 October 1962).

When the term ended, he went straight to Yugoslavia – which in 1962 had completed its separation from the Soviet bloc by becoming a founding member of the non-aligned movement with India and was fairly easy for a Westerner to access. The trip was hideous – he had summoned his courage to fly to Zurich, but the plane developed a fault and had to turn back – 'it is a tribute to the tranquillisers I had taken that I did not make myself ill with frenzy' (31 December 1962). There was no alternative flight, so he had to go back into London, and find a train to Paris, then another to Venice and a third to Belgrade, pausing at every change to send a telegram saying where he was and when he would arrive. In all, the trip took nearly three days, and the pair spent the next eleven days together, by the end of which 'we had agreed to marry – if this should be possible legally'. Francis, however, fell prey to his usual caveats: 'with so much subconscious hostility to the whole relationship, this has set doubts coursing through me ...' (31 December 1962).

Larissa also seems to have had her doubts, which manifested as 'severe palpitations of the heart, and mild recurrences of this during the next 10 days ...' (31 December 1962). She had other things to worry about as well: when she expected Francis to arrive by plane she went to the airport to meet him, but noticed that she was being watched. So she took a bus back to the city, got off halfway there, and hid down a side alleyway, noticing her follower peering out of the bus door into the gloom to try and see where she had gone. After Francis left, she was invited by the manager of her hotel for a game of chess. She found a KGB man waiting for her and had to listen while the manager then informed him officially that she had been seeing a lot of the Englishman. 'It was very honest of him to say all this with me there.' The KGB man – officially the representative of the Soviet air force in Yugoslavia – listened, shrugged, and said – 'It happens.' Larissa believed that he did not bother to report the matter back to Moscow: 'Such a kind man.'

Part of the reason Francis and Larissa got on so well was compatibility – physical, certainly, but equally in habits. Francis set a hard pace when travelling and indeed sometimes seems obsessive; since he first went to Italy, his diaries have accounts of long journeys on buses or often walking, through blistering heat and snowstorms or driving rain, scarcely pausing for lunch or rest, and all in pursuit of the next site he wanted to visit. Generally he did all this on his own because there were few who could match his enthusiasm or fortitude. On the grand trip around Sicily in 1953, he visited many places alone as his companion often preferred to rest in the hotel with a drink and a book. In Larissa he met his match at last: she had as many enthusiasms, and as much stamina. 'Our voyage to Kiev was a marvel. *Nonostante* 30 hours of travelling in a bus there and the same back and visiting 5–6 museums every day it was not so tiring ...' (LS to FH, 5 June 1964). The result was everything he had been looking for since his correspondence on the subject with George Cary in 1946: 'lovemaking

… was followed naturally by a visit to friends, an art gallery, the opera or shopping. This to me was a new and thrilling experience; love making coexisted with friendship, affection & respect' (29 September 1962). As he discovered when he began to visit her in Leningrad, in some areas she could outlast him: she could stay up until near dawn night after night, drinking, dancing and talking. A mere fortnight of such a schedule reduced him to near ruin, so much so that after a few years of marriage, he stopped going with her for her annual visit home. He simply couldn't take the pace.

Yugoslavia was a success but not because it was a particularly wonderful country to visit: in that he fully shared Larissa's opinion. He thought the quality of the cultural life was rather low – after a visit to the main art gallery in Belgrade he wrote: 'a fake Guardi … two fake Magnascos, a picture absurdly called Caravaggio … an ugly and much repainted Zanchi, a fake Fragonard. The average is rather high for a Jugoslav museum. Only about 85% of the pictures are totally lousy' (31 December 1962). But that did not matter; the exploration together made all the difference.

A harder test came when Francis went to Leningrad the following April, after concocting the excuse that it was imperative he study the collection of Tiepolo drawings at the Hermitage for his next book. This was no easy journey – he left London on Tuesday and arrived in Leningrad on Friday, taking a train to Harwich, a boat to the Hook of Holland, another train – with a 'special green coach' for Russia-bound passengers – to Berlin, then on to Warsaw, then Brest, then Moscow and finally to Leningrad, with lengthy stops at customs posts and Intourist offices along the way. Once he arrived and was ensconced in the Europa Hotel, he and Larissa had to behave with a suitable distance in public, and both were clearly unnerved by what they were doing.

Francis's diary was formal – 'I was taken around the collection by Larissa Salmina …' (6 April 1963) – and only when he got back safely to England did he write an account of his real impressions. Then he could give vent 'to the anxieties which were always in the background' when she told him that 'on her return from Belgrade all her luggage had been searched and one of my very compromising letters to her read aloud by a customs official'. There was a stark contrast between the overwhelming friendliness of the Russians he met and the background atmosphere of menace that pervaded all that he did and saw. This was not just official – after lunch with a friend of Larissa's who had been denounced by a colleague and sent off to the Gulag as a result, he realised 'how much private spite and rivalries could be indulged during the Terror – this far more than straight repression from the authorities'. But at the same time, Larissa's mother 'was as kind as if I had been a beloved son-in-law instead of a potentially dangerous foreigner'; her friend Marta 'a friendly, kind, shabby

Francis and Larissa, Leningrad, April 1963

girl'; Natasha – 'Larissa's husband's mistress' – 'a jolly, bouncy sexy girl, enormously friendly' (20 April 1963).

And there was the Hermitage, so gigantic and so rich in treasures it made him disoriented and almost ill from the realisation that he didn't know where to begin, and the wonders of the city itself with its palaces, churches, ballet, opera. For once in his life, he ran out of words:

> spent a good deal of time, in a rather frustrated sort of way, looking at pictures – but there are so many that I want to see, remember, make notes about, that I jump from one to another without being able to concentrate very much ... the number and quality is too rich to be able to choose or comment [on] with any ease.

In addition, the visit itself was a pleasure – few foreign academics came to the Hermitage, so he was treated as a much sought-after celebrity, and there was no trouble with conversation as many of the employees were old enough to pre-date the Revolution, had learned French as a matter of course in the way that the Imperial elite did, and had even travelled to the West before that became difficult.

This oscillation between wonder and love, fear and foreboding, marked the entire visit, even for Larissa, who told him as he prepared to leave that halfway through his stay,

> she had been summoned to the police station and asked all about me: where did I have all my meals? What were my aims in coming to Russia? What were my political views? (Typical, said Larissa, of the English Intelligentsia.) What did we talk about together? Love? Larissa sensibly told the entire truth except for the fact of our love affair ... she is

rather relieved at this denouement. It's out in the open now. If they trust her enough to ask that sort of question, it's a good sign, etc. But her mother naturally has been terribly frightened and I'm ashamed to say that – without showing it – I privately got into an egoistic panic as well as being terribly worried for her.

These worries – the fear of surveillance, discovery, retribution – were an integral part of the Cold War, now heightened by the intensifying reaction in the Soviet government to Khrushchev's vulnerability. Even Larissa had to take notice of it, and on a trip to Peterhof – Peter the Great's answer to Versailles on the coast to the south-west of Leningrad – they had 'a terribly pessimistic conversation – Larissa talking of the possibility, the likelihood, of a return to Stalinism: all so incongruous amid such serene beauty' (20 April 1963).

That discomfort did not quench his own curiosity, however. The period in which they met was, as far as England was concerned, the great age of the spy – the first Bond film and Len Deighton's *Ipcress File* came out in 1962, le Carré's *The Spy Who Came in from the Cold* in 1963. This public fascination was turbocharged by a series of scandals which had been rocking the British establishment from 1951, when Guy Burgess and Donald Maclean defected, to 1963 and the defection of Kim Philby.[5] It came to a natural finale in 1989, with the public exposure of Francis's friend Anthony Blunt. In between were countless episodes which suggested that the Soviet Union had infiltrated deep into British society and government, and that the security services were incompetent, amateurish and compromised. The story of this period is well enough known already, but Francis's role as observer adds an interesting sidebar to the tale. He was a member of the Apostles, the Cambridge debating society which managed to include serving members of both the Soviet and British secret services at the same time, and so moved in the same circles and imbibed many of the same values.

The emotional ties that linked the Apostles were very strong; to a considerable extent they did see themselves as belonging to a Society within society, and loyalties sometimes conflicted. The raison d'être was nominally intellectual, but while English society excelled at social clubs and networks, it was never very adept at the type of intellectual salons that France could produce. A rival to the Apostles had been the Souls, supposedly formed to generate serious discussion from the 1880s onwards, but which quickly became 'a group of men and women bent on pleasure, but pleasure of a superior kind ... looking for ... excitement in romance and sentiment'.[6]

The Apostles tried to be more serious. Its meetings were far from sinister – Francis's accounts are of evenings that were little more than someone reading an essay of considerable self-importance, followed by discussion, and book-ended by sherry and sardines on toast. Membership was all male and meetings took place in the college rooms of E. M. Forster. It was resolutely generalist – nothing technical, nothing scientific, only amateur philosophy. But the members most certainly saw themselves – in a polite sort of way – as the cleverest of all, rose to places of influence, and kept in contact with each other. New members were recruited in the same way that the security agencies then approached potential recruits – spotted by another member, interviewed at a party without being aware of it, then quietly offered membership. Until he was elected himself, Francis didn't even know it existed. As it was intergenerational – old members long past their student days frequently turned up and discussions were deliberately egalitarian – the young men went into the world with a ready-made patronage network, and learned in time to be similarly helpful to those who came afterwards. Certainly, Francis benefitted, and particularly from the friendship and support of Noel Annan, one of the most influential people of his generation.[7]

This sense of belonging to a mutually reinforcing elite meant that when Francis left Larissa and returned to Moscow to get the train home, he saw nothing wrong in filling in the spare time there by going to the birthday party of Guy Burgess, the fellow Apostle whose defection had begun the era of national outrage and soul-searching. He had fled along with another spy, Donald Maclean, who was on the brink of being arrested. Burgess had sent so much material to the Soviet Union over the previous decade that the only reason it seems to have done little damage was that the sheer quantity made the Russians suspicious it might be a cunning British plot to feed them misinformation. He had led a charmed life up to his departure and one similar to Francis's own – Eton, Cambridge, the Apostles, then a stint on the fringes of the world of politics. Thereafter, their paths diverged – the war took Burgess, a committed Communist since university, into the diplomatic service and then intelligence – which was exactly what his Russian controllers wanted.

No outsider ever thought Burgess was an appealing character – the *Guardian* described him later as a 'smelly, scruffy, lying, gabby, promiscuous, drunken slob', and it was much more generous than other newspapers. But for those in or near his social circle, he was seen as having charm and charisma – Noel Annan placed him in the same category as Francis's friend Simon Raven as a 'liberator', his behaviour and cruelty in conversation freeing others from 'the shackles of family, school or class'.[8] His contacts protected him at every turn; when he joined MI6 he was not even vetted, as his new employers assumed that his background – similar to their own – was a sufficient guarantee. He had been in his Russian exile for twelve years and detested the place by the time Francis met him, accompanied by Mark Frankland, a mutual friend, another member of the Apostles, the Moscow correspondent for the *Observer* and also a former (the KGB assumed still-serving) member of MI6. Francis later terrified Anthony Blunt – not yet unmasked but aware he was under suspicion with his telephone tapped – by ringing him up when he returned to England and cheerfully telling him that 'Guy sends his love'.

Francis's account of the birthday party in Moscow is curious, to say the least:

At 7 we went to dinner with Guy Burgess. He has a very comfortable flat, several rooms lined with books and pictures – Cezanne reproduction, El Greco copy, Henry Moore drawing, etc. He was slightly drunk (it was his birthday and he had been given a huge Russian lunch, but it is apparently not true that he is always drunk – he has an ulcer), and was wearing a white shirt, loose at the bottom to reveal a very fat paunch, and an OE [Old Etonian] tie. He has great charm, was extremely genial, and was anxious to talk about English friends and acquaintances – Anthony Blunt, Ellis Waterhouse, Dadie (Rylands), Victor Rothschild etc – and the past; very often scandalous and highly uncommunist: ie the time that so-and-so got drunk in Monte Carlo and picked up a sailor. Only very rarely did he get serious: he talked a lot, and obviously felt a great sense of guilt about 'sending Julian Bell to his death in Spain.'[9]

Of all the people he knew, it was Morgan [E. M. Forster] whom he said would most alarm him to meet now – his 'integrity' (he is trying to get him translated, but said the Russians don't approve of the religious elements in *Passage to India*) ... He said repeatedly 'I'm not a <u>Russian</u> Communist,' and obviously doesn't care much for the Russians or Russian life ... it was memories and old time gossip that he really enjoyed – he is obsessed with the past and with England, reads everything in the *Times* every day, *New Statesman*, *New Yorker* ('did you see Wystan's [Auden's] article on Wilde?'), *Literary Supplement*, etc. We had an excellent dinner – he ate nothing – prepared by his housekeeper: soup, grouse, ice cream with hot chocolate sauce, Georgian wine ... After dinner, his boyfriend (Russian-speaking only) came in – genial, broad shoulders, stolid, a factory worker – very unlike the usual type (ie Angus' [Wilson's], Anthony's [Blunt's]), though Mark said he was very much on best behaviour and can be flirtatious. We also talked a lot about the Society: he was all for keeping out Catholics. What about Communists, I asked? The evening was a huge success, and we stayed until 11.30, he implored me to come again if I ever return to Moscow. I think he is pretty bored and lonely. (20 April 1963)

The account is interesting not least because it is possibly the last view of Burgess, who died some four months later of arterio-sclerosis and liver failure. The following year, Francis went to the annual dinner of the Apostles, where speakers delivered affection-ate eulogies:

And last night the Society dinner at Bertorelli's[10] ... inter-esting mainly because of Noel's speech – excellent; humane, humorous, v. sympathetic about Guy Burgess (So much nicer than Guy himself, who I remember in Moscow was rather bitchy about Noel): 'What he enjoyed more than anything else was going to bed with boys ... dirty, filthy fingernails, etc, a Soviet agent, betrayed his country and his friends, but in some ways the Society really was at the centre of his life.'

(This is true, as I can confirm). Denis Proctor spoke next[11] – had been one of his closest friends, etc: Guy went over because he wanted to warn Russia about danger of war – Korea, MacArthur and so on. Had never been Soviet agent. His deep admiration for Morgan Forster (who was there, and purred: this too I can confirm). His (Denis') emotions at Noel's speech. And others to the same effect. It was rather an inspiring occasion, the thing I love best about England – a certain moral courage required, as all these people were members of the 'establishment:' I'm sure it was the obituary that would have meant most to Guy. (n.d. June 1964)

The newspapers would not have been so generous had a report of this dinner ever come to their attention and would not have seen the eulogies as moral courage. But the account does high-light the degree to which this part of the establishment was indeed detached from the rest of the country, as the press (and novelists like le Carré) tended to believe. The uproar over the Cambridge spies in the outside world was long-lasting and profound in its effects, but in Francis's circle it meant remarkably little, and never did: according to Larissa, 'everybody knew' that Anthony Blunt – who had helped Burgess escape in the 1950s and was made to confess to MI6 in 1964 only a few weeks before this dinner took place – was a Soviet agent. Blunt was given immunity from pros-ecution, allowed to continue as Keeper of the Queen's Pictures, and only after he was publicly exposed in 1979 did some express disapproval and stop inviting him for dinner.

———

Francis was worried when he left Russia that it would be a long time before he ever saw Larissa again, but in fact they met once more a few months later, and once more in Venice. This was a scheme which originated with their mutual friend Sandro Bettagno, who had introduced them and who found the role of matchmaker a pleasant one, although he could be alarmingly indiscreet: 'I've received the letters from Bettagno where he writes quite openly about us ... can you imagine?' (LS to FH, 7 June 1963). He concocted a plan for an exhibition of Venetian drawings at the Fondazione Cini and approached Alexei Adzhubei, a journalist passing through Venice who was married to Khrushchev's daughter Rada, to help him borrow drawings from the Hermitage. Larissa was the obvious person to organise the Russian end and write the catalogue, although it was not clear at first that she would be assigned to take them to Italy: 'the exhibition of our Venetian drawings appears to be in September in Venice ... but I am far from being sure that I would be allowed to go there' (LS to FH, 2 June 1963). She was ultimately approved, but the expedition was not nearly as pleasurable as before: Bettagno's chronic lack of organisation nearly ended Larissa's career and put a question mark over whether she would ever be allowed to leave the Soviet Union again.

The problem was that he scheduled the exhibition to open in the autumn of 1963, but when Larissa arrived with the drawings on 18 September, he announced that he had made a mistake and had organised another exhibition for the same time, and so there would have to be a delay. Larissa was quite happy with this – spending an extra few weeks in Venice at the expense of the Soviet government was not the worst outcome, but she didn't know what to do with the 127 drawings by Bellini, Titian, Bassano, Veronese, Tiepolo and Tintoretto that she had brought with her. So (this was truly a different age) she put them in a box under the bed in her *pensione*, where they stayed for the next month. She also wrote to Francis to see if he could come as well. But the delays continued – in fact, the exhibition did not open until the following March – and Larissa began to get careless, travelling around Italy again in defiance of the rules, especially when Francis turned up for a fortnight, which for him was 'a marvellous surprise after the depression and flatness I felt after my return from America' (7 October 1963). He had just been on his first lecture tour, and had not enjoyed the experience much – he loved the landscape, but disliked the cities, hated the flying, and found the remorseless politeness of the Americans deeply unsettling. Larissa was meanwhile becoming increasingly irritated with the Italians, particularly their carefree approach to organisation:

The end of my patience with the Fondazione has come. I am really furious. Now they must do really very little to finish my catalogue, nobody pays any attention to it. Besides, my *permesso di soggiorno* is over and nobody does anything to renew it … I don't know what to do at all … (LS to FH, 20 October 1963)

When Bettagno told her of the delay to the exhibition, Larissa had contacted the Hermitage asking how to proceed, and was told by Mikhail Artamonov, the director, to sit tight and under no circumstances leave the drawings behind: 'he agrees to my staying here – at any rate I can take it as a justification, because I haven't received an answer from anyone else' (LS to FH, 16 October 1963). But, of course, she hadn't asked anyone else, nor did Artamonov notify the authorities in Moscow, who began to worry that not only did they have a defector on their hands, she might have absconded with the pick of the Hermitage's collection of drawings as well. Soon after she received the telegram from

Leningrad telling her to stay put, she got a phone call from the embassy in Rome: 'they told me that the Ministry (of Culture) is furious, that the prolongation I received from our director was worth nothing and that I must immediately return. Rather a "nice" surprise which at once made everything very black ...' (LS to FH, 27 October 1963). It took her some time to decide what to do, and in the end she split the difference – she returned to Russia but left the drawings behind at the Fondazione Cini. She also took an entirely unjustifiable detour via Paris, concocting a need for an overnight stay before a connecting flight to Moscow, and in all delayed her return by nearly three weeks after being told to come back immediately.

But she had always wanted to see Paris, especially as it was easy for Francis to come and join her one more time. For Francis,

the whole brief stay together seems like a trance. We went rapidly round the Louvre, had a drink in the Café de la Paix, a good dinner in the Régence (where Max took me just after the war – I have never been back since out of a sort of reverence; but this occasion was important enough – and how he would have approved!) (10 November 1963)

But he did not feel it was the mutual introduction either Larissa or Paris, two loves of his life, deserved – 'I was able to show her virtually nothing' – and he came back worried about her future: 'she is in trouble, in danger, even ... God knows what her situation is at this moment, while I sit in my warm and comfortable room with Falstaff on the gramophone ...' (10 November 1963).

He was right to be concerned, as she was immediately summoned to the Ministry of Culture, where she was savagely criticised for disobeying orders. Fortunately, Artamonov's telegram ordering her to stay at least gave her some cover, but the alarm she had caused meant that she was not entirely forgiven. Even worse, the Hermitage decided to put the exhibition on itself after it closed in Venice in May 1964, and so wanted the drawings returned quickly. Bettagno offered to bring them back himself, but the Fondazione Cini would not pay for him to go; nor would the Hermitage send anyone from Russia. So they simply had them posted but skimped on the costs again. The box was packed properly but, by the time it was delivered, it had evidently been manhandled and spent time stacked on railway platforms in the rain. When Larissa collected it, she was shocked: 'I was in Moscow to pick up our drawings and they are not in a good condition' (LS to FH, 24 February 1965). In fact, they were so badly damaged that many needed urgent restoration. It was a fitting end to a disastrous episode, especially as the KGB representative at the Hermitage then told Larissa that, as far as he was concerned, she would never be allowed to leave Russia again.

This debacle seems to have been the last straw for Artamonov, who had been an irritant to the authorities for much of his thirteen-year tenure. He had made a point of employing people coming back from the Gulag, such as the historian and anthropologist Lev Gumilev;[12] had refused to hand over Hermitage treasures for the government to give away to visiting dignitaries; and at the same time that he instructed Larissa to stay in Venice, he was engaged in a fierce fight with the Ministry of Culture, the Party and the Academy over the value of modern art. Soon after Larissa returned from Venice in 1964, the forces ranged against him became too great and he was fired, with hundreds of museum staff lining the steps in tribute as he left the building. He was replaced by his deputy, Boris Piotrovsky, a fellow archaeologist who made a show of refusing to take the post for a full month, before accepting out of fear that some Party apparatchik might get the job instead. The handover was, perhaps, not as friendly as it seemed: when Larissa was being interrogated by the Party committee at the Hermitage after her marriage, 'Artamonov ... and Gumilev came up to me. They said, "Did we hear correctly that you married a foreigner?" I replied, "Yes." They realised how much trouble this would cause Piotrovsky and started dancing in the corridor!'

Like most at the Hermitage, Larissa deeply admired Artamonov, but was equally concerned about what his removal meant for her own position, and the outlook wasn't good. Not only was life in general progressively becoming more constrained, she also now faced the prospect of being banned from travelling to the West, at least for a while, and only being able to see Francis if he came to visit her. He did travel to Leningrad again in 1964, but this time he came back gloomy and despondent, not least because he was beginning to understand fully how risky the whole relationship was becoming. Larissa and a colleague took him back to Peterhof. It was a lovely day,

But the chauffeur was a surly man ... and when we got back to the hotel, he insisted on coming in so that he could 'denounce them for having passed over military secrets to a foreigner' ... Even the ugly and glum looking man (ostensibly the Astoria Intourist agent) to whom it was made could not take it seriously ... but it was obviously upsetting to Larissa and her friend. (25 April 1964)

# Departure and Arrival, 1965

*Negotiating a Marriage – Francis Pulling Strings – Help from
the KGB – Larissa Denounced – The Palace of Marriages –
Witness Sent to Siberia – Quest for a Passport –
Help from MI5*

On 27 June 1965 a despairing Francis began to write an account
'for the sake of historical record – to show what it is like in 1965 to
try and marry a Russian …' He was soon to set off for Leningrad
for the second time that year, on a trip which would end either in
triumph or in tragic disappointment. And it would not become
clear until the very last moment which it would be.

If Larissa said that she had fallen almost instantly in love with
Francis, her activities suggested a certain indecision. Not that she
was not in love; rather, the consequences were so daunting, even
if any long-term relationship was possible at all. So, in between
meeting Francis and divorcing her husband, she had what she
archly described as a 'fling' with an old fellow student from the
Academy of Fine Arts, an architect called Alexei Bilitin whom
she had known for years but had lost sight of until she returned
from Venice. It was never particularly serious – not least because
Bilitin had both a wife and a mistress already, and Larissa was

married and in love with Francis. But he was fun and charming and handsome, and she enjoyed herself with him. She was careful, however, not to mention any of this to Francis in her letters: 'there was so much I couldn't tell him ...'

This little episode highlights one of the fundamental differences between them: just as Francis's openness to the idea of marriage most certainly had much to do with his new financial situation fitting his fundamentally bourgeois belief that it was a husband's task to provide for his wife, so he was highly conventional on the subject of fidelity – while he was attracted in theory to the loose mores of Bloomsbury, he could never adopt them with conviction himself. Larissa, in contrast, had never come across such a thing before: her uncle, her mother, all of her colleagues and all of her friends had frequent affairs, and often multiple husbands and wives as well, often simultaneously. Nothing surprised her more than the realisation that she was about to get married to someone who was completely monogamous. She had not expected it and simply assumed that he would continue to have affairs. So when Francis sailed back across the Atlantic after a lecture tour in Canada in 1964 with Anne Wollheim, the wife of the philosopher Richard Wollheim, Larissa naturally enquired whether she had been good in bed. Francis was flabbergasted and utterly appalled: 'she expresses jealousy for my trip abroad: who with, etc. Darling Larissa, don't let's give ourselves unnecessary pain ...' (3 October 1964). It didn't give Larissa any pain at all, and she found his response so funny she couldn't help occasionally teasing him about it: after he went for lunch in Venice with Anna-Maria Cicogna, she wrote, 'Poor darling, I shan't be jealous of her and will allow you to see her alone if you like ...' (14 September 1965).

If that hints at some uncertainty on her part about the wisdom of pursuing the relationship with Francis, he was similarly anguished for a long time. The diaries are full of doubts and worries, and echoes of his old defences – for some time he was convinced that she was far more in love than he was, which merely goes to show that self-knowledge often eludes even the most intelligent and self-examining of people. In fact, he was clearly besotted from the moment they met, and only became more so as the months and years passed. But he did have to do some adjusting, not least to Larissa's self-perception honed by 'the Russian aim to treat all women as intellectual equals' (8 April 1965); although in this case, while he was able to adapt, the society in which he asked Larissa to live was not.

If the prospect of leaving Russia was a giant step into the unknown for Larissa, the prospect of marriage was in a way equally so for Francis, as it meant leaving the secure familiarity of his entire life to that point. He had never lived on his own and had spent twenty-six of his then thirty-seven years communally in institutions – sent away from home at 8 to prep school, then to Eton, the army, and King's as both undergraduate and fellow. The rest of the time had been spent with his parents or with families as a paying guest, with all domestic duties attended to by others; even when he shared a flat in Rome with Sandro Marabottini, the Italian had insisted on having a maid. He knew nothing of even the basics of living. He had never had a kitchen. He had never done any routine shopping or laundry and had never learned to drive. Cooking was a complete mystery – although it was for Larissa as well, as her mother prepared all meals for her at home. When she did arrive in England, the new couple racked up formidable bills as she would phone Vera for instructions every time she tried to prepare something beyond the most basic.

Francis had learned sociability, but not intimacy. The two were mutually incompatible: to survive in a boarding school or a Cambridge college it is necessary to develop a form of distant affability, to be collegial and cooperative, but no more. Closeness is dangerous, it breeds factionalism, and a falling out or emotionally charged argument in the closed confines of such a place can blow it apart, as people are stuck with each other whether they like it or not. The option of no longer seeing or talking to the other person does not exist. To live in common requires a certain coolness and wariness; it defined Francis's social world, and is the fundamental reason he found leaving the country both a relief and a necessity. In his England it was never truly safe to be absolutely open with others: this, at least, was something he understood about Larissa's life in Russia.

But everything which makes life in common possible is fatal for an intimate relationship. There trust is central, openness essential. To take the risk of being hurt, to discard the protective layers of distance and affability in favour of real emotion was, for Francis, difficult, and indeed terrifying. He had never done it before – not with his friends, with his siblings, with his parents, not even with his occasional lovers, and he didn't know if he could. He knew that he would miss much of his old life – what he termed 'the pull of easy, man-to-man bachelorhood' (27 October 1963). And the fear kept nagging at him: coming back from Paris he wrote of 'a certain concealed longing to escape … into a more familiar background' (25 December 1963). A few months later he noted that 'drinks in the pub … have become such a regular ritual that I will feel utterly lost when it all comes to an end' (28 February 1964). One of his most potent fears as he and Larissa became ever closer was what would happen if she abandoned everything, and he then found that he could not deliver his side of the deal and make it worth her while – precisely what Larissa herself had thought of as a possibility: 'it's no use pretending that even now I'm yet certain that a marriage would really work. But, God knows, I want to try …' (22 April 1964).[1]

Marriage, or at any rate an attempt to get married, was not inevitable; for some time in fact it seemed unlikely. Neither initially considered it a viable option and the pattern they had established – Larissa wangling trips to the West, Francis manufacturing reasons to study Italian drawings at the Hermitage – worked reasonably well and seemed a fair compromise between their desire to be together and the reluctance to upend their lives and careers. His friend Mark Frankland even suggested they get married with Larissa then staying in Russia and Francis visiting as often as possible. This might have suited Frankland, but it did not appeal to Francis in the slightest.

Also, Khrushchev's fall, and the trouble that Larissa found herself in after the debacle with the drawings, made her realise that their options were shrinking fast. The death of her father in 1961 and, in late 1964, the death of her patron and supervisor Mikhail Dobroklonsky loosened her emotional ties to the status quo and made her position more tenuous. The prospect of years of agreeable meetings in the pleasanter parts of Europe began to fade. Very quickly the options resolved into a simple choice – get married or give up. They had to make up their minds quickly; there was the usual interregnum after Khrushchev was deposed in October 1964, and if she were going to try and leave it would have to be done before the new regime got its hands firmly on the levers of power.

All of this was decided during Francis's Leningrad trip of March–April 1965. Larissa would try to get permission to leave the Soviet Union. There was no question, however, of anything that might resemble a defection. Such a step would have meant total severance from her mother, her friends and her life in Leningrad. She would never have been allowed back and those closest to her would have been vulnerable to retribution. She wished to leave because it was necessary to be with Francis, not because of any disaffection for the Soviet Union, and that meant having to get married inside Russia first, doubling the number of bureaucratic hoops they would have to jump through, with the possibility of failure at every stage: 'there are agonising risks in our policy of action' (6 April 1965).

One problem had been solved already by the death of Larissa's father; she grieved for him terribly, but it opened the way for her to marry. Adult Russians were legally responsible for their parents in old age. Permission to leave the country depended on parents waiving their rights to be looked after. Vera, who liked Francis and was desperate for her daughter to find happiness, willingly did this: it may have appealed to her own sometimes reckless approach to life. Certainly, it was an extraordinarily generous gift to her daughter. But Larissa was certain her father would have refused: 'He would never have allowed me to go abroad to marry Francis. He disliked all foreigners and was very nationalistic.' Her uncle was more broad-minded about foreigners, but 'just thought it was wrong to marry one'. Fortunately, he had no means of preventing the marriage and was perfectly polite about it when he finally met Francis. Shortly before the wedding, he even organised a long dinner for him with a dozen aged relatives. As none of these spoke anything but Russian, communication was conducted solely through the medium of encouraging smiles and vodka, leaving Francis very much the worse for wear.

To organise the marriage, Larissa ruled out a direct approach in Russia as too risky: 'Rather than the authorities in Leningrad ... which would apparently result in immediate uproar, she wants me to make such arrangements as I can through the Russian embassy in London ...' (28 March 1964). Francis therefore returned to England with the task of mobilising every possible contact he had assembled over the years at school, university and beyond. He began to lay the groundwork in June, writing, 'I'm now going to see Noel [Annan] and try to work things out at a high level' (4 June 1964), and Annan wrote to Sir Harold Caccia, the senior civil servant at the Foreign Office, for advice. The response was not encouraging: Annan reported that 'Caccia thinks that any intervention at a high level would be useless and possibly harmful' (30 April 1964), advice which directly contradicted that of Larissa herself. He also consulted Mark Frankland, who directed him to an English émigré in Moscow – a man Francis found simultaneously unhelpful and unpleasant. And finally, the historian Orazio Pugliese suggested making an approach through the Italian Communist Party, an idea Francis rejected as 'I am doubtful if this would work and hate any politicisation of the affair' (10 July 1964).

In other words, his collection of friends and contacts had failed: there was no way to get through to people of sufficient importance in the Soviet Union in a fashion that would make any positive difference. So, almost in desperation, Francis consulted his father. This was not something he wanted to do – being dependent on Arnold did not make him comfortable in any way; he only told him of Larissa's existence at the beginning of 1965. But his father responded better than he had ever expected. The conversations between the two had always been about art and music, never about emotions. Arnold often pried into Francis's life, was proud of his accomplishments, but never showed any interest in his feelings: in that respect, he didn't really know his son at all. But this new matter was practical and played to the older man's strengths. Besides, it was undoubtedly flattering to have a son so precisely following in his own footsteps by falling in love with a Russian, even if he missed the fact that Francis's greatest desire was to create a marriage as different to his parents' as was possible.

Arnold offered to open his own address book, and as he was deeply embedded in the world of ballet, which was so completely dominated by Russia, he had many people to choose from. After some thought, he decided on perhaps the most dangerous person imaginable, a man called Vsevolod Nikolaevich Sofinsky, the cultural attaché at the Soviet Embassy whom he knew as an ardent enthusiast for ballet.[2] Sofinsky had been to the family home for drinks, was amiable and knowledgeable, but, Arnold told his son, was 'of no great influence'. That was not true, and Arnold was certainly worldly enough to know it, but as Larissa said, 'Francis's father was very vain and easily courted.' In reality, Sofinsky was the head of the KGB station in London and had more than enough influence to wreak havoc had he so chosen. Even for Arnold, getting to see him was not easy – Sofinsky cancelled and cancelled again, each time sending Francis into a paroxysm of suspicion.

Just in case this line of attack fizzled out, Arnold prepared a letter to a contact from the Moscow Festival Ballet, Yekaterina Furtseva, the Minister of Culture. If anything, this was still more risky. Furtseva was powerful enough to be helpful if she chose. But she was weakening – unpopular with the incoming regime, she had also fallen out with Khrushchev. Besides, she was known for pursuing vindictive campaigns against those who displeased her. As Larissa fell well within her sphere of influence because of her job at the Hermitage, it was probably for the best that the letter was never sent.

But eventually the meeting with Sofinsky took place and Arnold made his pitch: 'The point of no return – daddy is at this moment talking to the Russian embassy man. I pray to whatever God there is that this doesn't cause her any misery ...' (10 May 1965). In fact, Sofinsky seemed to be sympathetic – hardly enthusiastic about the prospect but not evidently hostile either – and promised to do what he could to help. He kept his word. Sofinsky – whose real job became public knowledge when, as Ambassador

Vsevolod Sofinsky in 1980

to New Zealand in 1980, he was caught handing a briefcase of cash to some Communists in Auckland – told Arnold how to proceed, instructed the Soviet consulate in London to cooperate and cleared a path back in Moscow for the couple. Francis then followed up with a visit to the consulate on 13 May: 'I called on Roschin, a bland, tough, good-looking, faceless man ... he told me, more or less, what papers I would need, said that he would write to the authorities ... I sent Sofinsky my book ...' After a series of nightmarish attempts to phone Larissa – one of which had him waiting on the line for two hours because her mother was having a marathon chat with a friend at the other end – he finally sent a telegram: 'Good news.'

Larissa was reassured, but apprehensive:

When it came I felt so frightened and happy at the same time
... I went to the marriage office and asked for terms: it seems
to be all right ... I am really sure that if there is a moment
when our marriage is possible it is now and I hope nothing
will change. (Letter, about 20 May 1965)

The date was set for sometime in July, but first Francis needed
to sort out the paperwork in England – above all, having the banns
read in order to obtain a 'certificate of no impediment', a document saying he was single, to present to the Soviet authorities in due
course. This required a public notice to be put up in the Shire Hall
of Cambridge for three weeks – a trivial legal necessity normally,
except that he feared it might be spotted by reporters who routinely
checked for titbits to put in the local paper. This was concerning
because part of Arnold's pitch to Sofinsky had been that neither of
the couple wanted to cause any fuss or had any desire to politicise
their marriage. Reports in newspapers along the lines of 'Russian
woman seeks to flee Soviet Union through marriage with don' could
easily have been interpreted as an attempt to cause embarrassment.

Then there were long visits to the embassy and the now genial
Roschin to sort out the visa, and booking the trip. Unfortunately
for Francis the dates of travel coincided with 'International
Friendship Week' – invented in Paraguay in the 1950s but taken
up by the Soviet Union with enthusiasm – which meant that most
of the trains were already full. Everything was eventually organised – transport booked, hotel room reserved, certificates and visa
obtained and stamped by both Russians and British – but he was
always aware that all the effort might be for nought: 'in cases such
as this it is the last rather than the first step that counts, and I am
feeling as uncertain as ever' (27 June 1965).

The wheels had been set irrevocably in motion. The Russian
authorities now knew Larissa wished to leave the Soviet Union,

and Francis had constant reminders that this could be dangerous. As he was preparing to leave, the newspapers were full of the story of a Swedish teacher, Stig Hansson, who wished to marry a Russian teacher. Not only did the Soviet authorities prevent this, they arrested his 32-year-old fiancée, Galina Petrovskaya, had her fired from her job, and then sentenced her to five years in a labour camp for living a 'parasitic and anti-social way of life'. At almost the same time, on 25 April 1965, an Englishman called Gerald Brooke was arrested in Moscow and charged with spreading anti-Soviet propaganda. Unlike another Englishman, Greville Wynne, who was arrested and jailed in 1962, Brooke was not even a real spy, although he did take in some illicit material. He was sentenced to five years' hard labour and did not get back to Britain until 1969. *Pravda* noted the deterrent effect: 'Brooke's example ought to help such "gentlemen" to adopt a more careful attitude' (23 July 1965). It was not only Larissa who was taking a risk.

Another report was even more depressing, if possible, as the Soviet authorities cancelled at the last moment the wedding of a librarian called Ludmilla Bibikova who wished to marry an Englishman called Mervyn Matthews, a student in Moscow who had formerly worked for the Foreign Office. This had already been a nightmare: when they had announced their engagement, Matthews was promptly arrested and expelled from the country on grounds of financial speculation and (again) of spreading anti-Soviet propaganda. The move caused a fuss, and questions were put in the House of Commons to the then Foreign Secretary Rab Butler, who made it clear that, while the government disapproved of the expulsion, it was not at all interested in the interrupted marriage or the stranded fiancée.[3] In other words, if the Soviet authorities turned hostile, neither Francis nor Larissa could expect any official assistance from Britain. They were on their own, and for both the penalties of any misjudgement could be dire.

So when Francis set off for Leningrad on 8 July he did not have his usual emotional uplift at the prospect of leaving England behind for a while:

> I'm in a more than usually jittery state ... the next few weeks are going to be Hell – Gerald Brooke is due to be tried for subversion while I am there ... emotion is subdued by worry, and I no longer know what I think about anything ... will we make it? (4 July 1965)

Even getting to the Soviet Union was difficult – and very expensive. The two trips Francis took in 1965 cost more than his entire annual salary, so that Larissa found herself in the same position as her own mother, who married Nikolai thinking that he was relatively well-off, only to discover that he had spent so much money wooing her that he was virtually penniless. Francis similarly had completely exhausted all his savings and gone into debt by the time Larissa arrived in England. Getting married in the Soviet Union was a lengthy business and required him to be in the country for several weeks beforehand to establish residency in Leningrad. The first trip of 1965, when they finally decided to take the plunge and notify the authorities, lasted for a fortnight, from 23 March to 6 April. The second took nearly six weeks, from 8 July to 14 August. Although many of the hotels were pretty dreadful – 'I stayed at the Ukraine, an absolutely odious hotel, a hideous Stalinist skyscraper of utter inefficiency' (26 April 1964) – they were not cheap: the Europa in Leningrad cost £12 a night, equivalent to nearly £200 in 2023. And getting there in the first place cost a fortune as well, quite apart from the time it took to get a visa of unusually long duration.

When Francis arrived, the first task the newly reunited pair had to complete was to go to the Leningrad Palace of Marriages to fill in the application form. 'Piped Strauss music, very heavy atmosphere. Delightful directress ... Possible, but not yet certain, seems verdict' (10 July). There were two more visits to the palace, two visits to the Interior Ministry, and one to Moscow for Francis to go to the British Embassy. For Francis, that was it; Larissa had a somewhat harder time as she was told she couldn't apply for an exit visa until she was married, and was periodically summoned by officialdom to be reprimanded.

> Larissa naturally suffered far more than I did and – equally naturally – fussed far less. She was twice summoned to some sort of ministry and on the first of these occasions was politely bullied and threatened (mother would have to give up flat, etc.) for four hours, though the second time the man was more conciliatory and had evidently been given instructions that the marriage was to be allowed to go through – perhaps after some message from Sofinsky in London ... (15 August 1965)

She was also called in by 'some high Party official who put on a great act of being mortally hurt (How could you, etc?)', as well as by the Hermitage Party secretary, 'who calmed down after an indignant outburst'.

After a couple of weeks, the paperwork was done, and they were given a date for the marriage ceremony. It was only four days before Francis's visa expired, so the entire stay was underpinned by anxiety that the wedding plans would collapse not because the marriage was forbidden, but merely because it was postponed. Francis, by now totally paranoid, was convinced it was a ruse, that the authorities were going to stop the marriage without having to forbid it openly.

But there was nothing further to be done except wait, and for Francis to plunge into the social life that was so much a part of

Larissa's world in Leningrad. He did not enjoy it as much. Try as he might – and he was on his very best behaviour – he simply did not have the stamina to stay up so late so often, to drink and eat quite so much. Night after night, with multiple visits to the theatre, opera and ballet as well ('The Senegalese ballet was disappointing, but the audience was thrilled by the bare breasts ...'[4]), combined with excursions to museums and architectural sights. When added to the underlying stress, Francis found it all overwhelming:

We saw a vast number of people, and there were constant parties, especially birthday ones ... usually with an elderly mother near the head of the table, lots of friends seated round, and endless piles of marvellous food and drink, the nearest thing to Dickensian celebrations I have ever come across, except that everyone is engaged in complicated love affairs and the dancing was hardly very 19th century.

There was also the business of going round to individual friends to tell them what was happening: Larissa's old boyfriend Evgeny Lubo-Lesnichenko 'was exceptionally warm', while her friend Marta was 'bitterly upset that Larissa was leaving ... As it was, she only cried a lot and, thank God, went away with her overwhelmingly possessive mother on holiday.'

Eventually the day came, and at 7.45 in the evening of 10 August the pair, with their guests, arrived at the Palace of Marriages for the ceremony – if it were to happen. And there was indeed a hitch: the certificate of no impediment that Francis presented had Larissa's date of birth wrong. Realising this sent him into a panic: 'I spent most of Tuesday itself living on purple hearts, aspirins and vodka.' But the officials didn't mind, and this insouciance was interpreted as a good sign there was not going to be any problem:

The Palace of Marriages, 10 August 1965

it would have been a perfect – and perfectly legitimate – reason to stop the wedding had anyone been so inclined.

The ceremony itself Francis found an anticlimax, considering the worry and effort that had gone into arranging it:

> the officials were friendly and smiling, made short speeches to the effect that they hoped the sentiments that had brought us here today would last all our lives, but omitted the homily that we should behave as good Soviet citizens ... We then exchanged rings ... signed some documents followed by our

witnesses and were handed back our passports in to which the official notification was stamped, like some visa ...

It was the guests who provided much of the interest, particularly the witnesses. These had been hard to find, as most of Larissa's friends either disapproved of the marriage or were worried about getting involved. Ultimately she chose her old friend Natasha, who had long since got rid of Larissa's husband and was now having an ostentatious affair with the other witness, Roma, whom Larissa had known since her days camping out in Moscow and who also brought his wife to the ceremony. This created a bit of an atmosphere. Roma had joined the police and was now the equivalent of a chief inspector, but was prepared to stick his neck out on her behalf. There was a price to be paid for this show of friendship: 'He signed the document and was immediately transferred to Siberia and told he would never work in Leningrad again. He found Siberia so depressing he resigned. Through a friend who worked in the Mariinsky Theatre he got a job as a fireman there.'

After that there was the reception, provisioned by the Europa Hotel. It was a condition of entering Russia that visitors had to buy coupons in advance to cover the cost of food. These were expensive, and Francis had generally eaten at Larissa's flat and so had never used them. Ordinarily, they would have been money down the drain, but he was now well known to the hotel management, and in honour of the marriage they offered to swap the coupons for 'red and black caviar, lots of fish, meat, cakes vodka, champagne and Russian Riesling', all of which they delivered to Larissa's apartment. The result was 'a jolly party, with no speeches of any kind', especially as Larissa limited numbers by telling many of her relatives 'that I couldn't invite them because the KGB had forbidden it. My mother's sister never forgave me.' At the end of the reception, in the small hours of the following day, Francis went back, alone, to his hotel: 'a strange wedding night, but then it has been a strange wedding ...'

As it turned out, getting married was the easy part. In order for them to be together, Larissa needed an exit visa granting permission to leave the Soviet Union permanently but with the option of returning to visit. This took a further four months, with the constant possibility that the application would be denied. Certainly, the authorities went out of their way to make this as difficult, and as miserable, an experience as possible. Francis's contribution was to worry: he left Russia two days later, flew to Stockholm, on to Copenhagen, then Rome, and finally to Venice, before returning to Cambridge at the beginning of October. All the while he was writing and phoning Larissa, who was in turn sending off letters to wherever she thought he might be.

The news initially was cheerful: 'My dear <u>Husband</u>: Monday was quite exciting as everybody <u>knew</u>. I am now a sensation. I am terribly afraid it will spoil me' (LS to FH, 16 August 1965). That insouciance did not last very long, however. A fortnight later it was becoming clear that leaving was going to be difficult:

> The time is very tough for me ... I am not sleeping at night, can't eat, have pains in my stomach and so on ... I gave all the documents to the militia and I have had the Party reference. It was like a guilty verdict. I have to abandon my work and soon will be sitting at home without money ... but the most terrible of all is that I was told that a normal period to get a visa is six months. (LS to FH, 2 September 1965)

Not only did she have to get clearance to leave the country, there was a possibility she would be fired from the Hermitage and ceremonially stripped of her Party membership as well. Much of this wouldn't matter in the long run – she was likely to be let out unless there was some dramatic (but always possible) change in government attitude before she left – but it did matter to her. It was a bitter disappointment, as she wanted so much to leave on good terms, but instead had to endure a sort of ritual humiliation, a way of expressing their very real regret as well as a signal to those in power that they should not be held responsible. As far as she was concerned, everything she was doing was perfectly legal and when called up to various committees she made a point of saying so.

The director and the Party organisation were all accusing me. I didn't know why they were doing this. I thought they should write to the government and Central Committee of the Party, saying that they disagreed with their policy on allowing Russian citizens to marry foreigners. Why didn't they ask to return to Stalin's time when it was totally forbidden?

But her protests changed nothing. She was accused time and again of being a traitor, of being disloyal, of putting the Hermitage itself at risk, often by people she trusted and liked, although some came up to her privately and congratulated her, wished her well, and said how lovely her new husband was.

Nor could she just walk away from the Hermitage, as the process of handing authority over the drawings collection to others had to be completed, and she was the only person who could do this. So it went on, daily getting worse: 'I am not yet sacked but … in our asylum there are bad and serious changes' (LS to FH, 14 September 1965).

By 16 October, Francis was becoming ever more worried and consulted his father again. Arnold recommended going back to the KGB man in London, telling his son that: 'I suggest that I write to Sofinsky, as indeed he asked me to do, in a calm and non-desperate way, telling him at the same time about my trip to Paris, etc. Please let me know at once – he may go on leave or be transferred and then we have no friend at court' (Arnold Haskell to FH, 16 October 1964). Two days later, though, the visa to leave the Soviet Union came through – but now Larissa did not have the visa to enter Britain, because the papers she had filed in advance did not have her place of birth or the name of her first husband. This caused an anguished series of letters with Francis until it was sorted out. But when she did finally obtain both visas, she no longer had the passport to put them in – it had been handed in with her applications, and not returned.

At this point, Larissa could take no more: her job at the Hermitage had ended, but she was still going into the museum to try and finish her handover, even though the attacks continued. She wrote to Francis that 'I have had to leave my work and everything concerned with it was so painful, insulting, unjust and so on the same day I left I bought an aeroplane ticket to the south where my mother was … It did me a lot of good.' Ten days by the sea in the Caucasus brought Larissa back to sanity and when she returned she found that the storm in the museum had passed over as well: in her absence, everyone seemed to have finally accepted she was going to leave.

But actually getting out was still an issue because of the missing passport, so Arnold did finally contact Sofinsky, who made enquiries and wrote back on 10 December: 'at present they are drawing up her exit papers and I think you will see your daughter-in-law in this country in the near future'. Francis then wrote to the consul, Roschin, who promptly replied that 'I have already been informed by Mr Sofinsky about your trouble and we have taken the necessary steps in order to speed things up. I hope that your separation from your wife will not last long now …' (Roschin to FH, 7 December 1965).

These interventions worked. Larissa received the last bits of paper she needed on 23 December. She thought she would take the train, as that would mean more luggage, but Francis wanted her out before anyone could change their mind. He told her to forget the luggage and just get on the first available flight. On 30 December he went to the airport and collected her. She arrived with a single suitcase full of books and papers, a print by Dürer left to her by Dobroklonsky sewn into the lining of her coat, and 'one pair of shoes, a change of underwear and a skirt'.

After she arrived, Francis's friend Noel Annan, the head of King's College and another former intelligence officer, asked his old colleagues in MI5 to leave her alone. As obliging as the KGB had been, they did so. Larissa went to the Soviet Embassy

Larissa with Francis and Enzo Crea in Cambridge, a few hours after arriving in England, 30 December 1965

to register her presence and say thank you to the consul, Roschin. She also had dinner with Sofinsky in the Savile Club. She did not enjoy the last occasion; while Francis's father thought that the Russian was a genial fellow, Larissa – who had been detained and questioned on several occasions by then – knew a seriously powerful KGB man when she met one. She was terrified, and spent much of the evening locked in the toilet being sick.

Annan helped again a few weeks later when the new couple wanted a holiday travelling around Europe – difficult when all you have is a Soviet passport. He was close to Roy Jenkins, the newly appointed Labour Home Secretary, and invited him and Larissa to lunch. By the time it was finished, Jenkins had promised to sort out British citizenship for her.

Larissa herself was not hugely cooperative, however; not only was her new name spelled wrongly on the marriage certificate (Khaskell) she lied about the fact that she had been married before – to an officer in the navy – and declined once more to offer any proof of her divorce, as she had on the application for the entry visa. The Home Office was annoyed when it found all this out, concerned that she was not legally married at all, or at least not to her British husband, and baulked at the idea of issuing her a passport on this basis.

Larissa was unsympathetic: no, she really didn't have any divorce papers; what was more, she wrote back that she wouldn't even say who her husband had been. 'Before leaving Russia last month, I solemnly promised my first husband that under no circumstances would I mention his name, or refer to the fact of our marriage and therefore it is not possible to give all the details you require …'

This was followed by a tart letter to the Home Office from Francis, somewhat in the manner of a disappointed employer chiding a lazy servant:

I would be most grateful if you could do your very best not to add to the extreme strain that my wife and I have both had to undergo ... Both of us particularly wish to take a holiday on the continent when the university term ends here in a fortnight's time, and I would therefore be extremely grateful if the matter could be settled as soon as possible. (FH to Home Office, 25 February 1966)

This did the trick: the passport was issued on 15 March, exactly eleven weeks after Larissa's arrival, and they left for Sweden and Germany a few days later. Larissa was now officially one of Her Majesty's subjects, and transformed in her passport from Larissa Salmina, art historian and curator, into her new British identity as Larissa Haskell, housewife. Francis's father wrote to congratulate him: 'Bravo – as the French so rightly say, "c'est du vrai piston" – or is it "the old boy's network?" Anyhow, I have always been a great admirer of Jenkins ...' (Arnold Haskell to FH, 18 March 1966).

# Finale

A month or so after her arrival, now staying in a dingy, cold, poorly furnished flat in the back streets of Cambridge as married fellows were not allowed to live in college, Larissa had her first encounter with English academia, and her future life. Francis suggested she might come to a feast at King's, and she was keen to go. She didn't have many clothes, but as an experienced seamstress she cobbled together something suitable and, when the time came, the newly married couple set off.

She was a little surprised when her husband bade her farewell at the entrance to the hall, but she knew little of English ways. So she waited as other women arrived and were similarly abandoned. Meanwhile the husbands, in full academicals, processed into the grand hall. There was the Latin grace, the toasts, the fine wines from the cellar, the indifferent food.

And the wives were escorted up to the musicians' gallery once the choir – one of the finest in the country – had finished singing. There they were given a glass of sherry, and some sausage rolls and spent the next few hours gazing down with suitable reverence as their husbands ate and drank themselves into oblivion in the midst of the college silver, glinting in the candlelight.

Women were not allowed to eat with the men. It would have caused a scandal. Even thirty years later, some fellows of colleges in both Oxford and Cambridge would still threaten to walk out if a woman came to dinner. Their brains all wool, as George Cary had put it to Francis twenty years earlier, women spoiled the conversation and put the men off their food. Most of the fellows had received the same sort of education as Francis, but unlike him, many never threw off the consequences and instead embraced their misogyny as a defence of standards and civilisation.

The wives – housewives, librarians and schoolteachers for the most part – made polite conversation about children and schools and gardens, but quietly, so as not to attract attention to themselves.

Larissa told one that she had newly arrived from Russia.

'How lovely! You must be so glad to be free!' came the reply.

Larissa, who had years of experience being careful about what she said, gazed down at the men below, then back at the women.

'Oh, yes,' she replied. 'Very glad.'

---

And so this story comes to its end. It is not complete; more than half of Francis's life, nearly two-thirds of Larissa's, is left out and much could be written about their later years. But not here. This is neither a history nor a biography, but only a simple tale of two people from a world long ago who meet and fall in love. The oldest story in the world, always the same but always different.

The literature they both loved familiarised them with the idea that all stories need structure and a fitting ending, and in some ways they seem unconsciously to have fashioned their relationship around this belief. The most ordinary and commonplace conclusion to their initial meeting would have turned it into a fleeting encounter that petered out because of the difficulties of pursuing it any further. But the intensity of emotions generated could not have been allowed to end in such a meaningless way. A satisfying climax was required to give purpose to those years of worry and desire, and to the long road they had both travelled. And so they continued, travelling to secret meetings, writing their coded letters, trying to pick their way to some more suitable final act. The end had to be triumph or tragic failure. The first was preferable. The second was dreaded, but would at least have been fitting.

Larissa never managed to re-establish her career; being one of Europe's experts in Italian drawing, with abundant experience in putting on exhibitions and organising museums, counted for little in the Britain of the 1960s. She was a woman. She applied for many jobs but was never considered seriously for any of them. Initially she sank into a depression when she came to England: 'I could no longer see God.' But she was characterised above all by an extraordinary adaptability and resilience, and a striking detachment from the external signs of status and position which preoccupy most people in one way or another. Scholarly work mattered greatly, having a position was not so important – indeed not having one created far more opportunities for travel. So she recreated her old life in a different way; she became a specialist in the Russian art she once knew little about and catalogued the large collection of works at the Ashmolean in Oxford, and then at the Victoria and Albert Museum in London. She produced a catalogue of the work of Leonid Pasternak, the father of the novelist; acted as adviser to museums and dealers and auction houses; wrote innumerable articles and reviews for journals. Her study at home was slowly taken over by vast piles of correspondence from people around the world seeking her advice and expertise. Above all, the effort to ensure an amicable departure from her homeland paid off: she was able to return untroubled to Leningrad almost every year to visit her mother and her friends.

The greatest sadness was not having a child. Perhaps because of the starvation and trauma she experienced as she was entering puberty, it was impossible. Both she and Francis speculated before they were married about what they would do if she became

Natural habitat: I Tatti, Tuscany, *c.* 1970

pregnant; within a few years of her arrival in England it became clear this was never going to happen. What was a fortunate escape before they married became a bitter disappointment afterwards. 'We realised that our attempts to get pregnant spoiled our life together ... We stopped trying after that.' Instead, she made full use of the freedom that not having a permanent job or children provided: she and Francis continued the frenetic travelling that he had begun in the 1950s, and spent much of the year abroad, living within an extensive friendship network that ultimately spread far beyond Europe.

Francis moved to Oxford in 1967, where he stayed for the rest of his career as Professor of the History of Art. His many books and articles will probably be his main claim to being remembered. I have not mentioned them much here, because I do not feel that they were his finest achievement. Overcoming his insecurities, fears and depression, breaking out of the straitjacket constructed from his inherited attitudes to people and life – all this required a much greater effort and was a far more substantial accomplishment. He could have, and nearly did, become like so many others of his generation and background – the 'timorous bachelor don' of his fears (2 December 1962), ever lonelier and more misogynistic, increasingly focused on the daily gossip of academia, pouring ever more of himself into his work. It would have been an emotional half-life, albeit stable in its narrowness, outwardly enviable and with its own rewards. He knew instinctively that it would bring him no real happiness, and he struggled for years to find an alternative by trying to understand himself. When that alternative turned up for dinner in a Venetian restaurant, he found the strength to shove aside all his timidity and anxiety to ensure the chance did not slip through his fingers. A few months after he met her, reflecting on their first night in Trieste, he wrote, 'I wonder if that night ... may yet save my life' (31 December 1962).

It did. And there is no better indication than the fact that, shortly after Larissa arrived in England, he stopped writing the diary which had been his most faithful friend for the previous two decades, and never took it up again. He no longer needed it. He had a far better companion to talk to.

# Postscript

Larissa died shortly after the manuscript of this book was completed. Fortunately, she quite enjoyed reading about herself ('I didn't realise I had been so indiscreet'), even though I had decided to stick to the facts and not add any of the more fanciful embellishments she would occasionally try to sneak into the story. Writing about her was an unusual experience. I began as a historian of the eighteenth century, then went on to fiction. Everyone I had ever written about was either long dead or invented. I had never before had one of my characters peering over my shoulder and commenting on my efforts. But she was a remarkably easy-going subject and, once it was clear that I was not going to allow Francis to take over and become the focal point of the narrative, made no attempt to control what I said.

It was terribly sad to lose her. I developed a great fondness and admiration for her in the time I spent taking her story down. But she chose her end. Although generally in robust good health, she was 93 and found life in the care home she moved into after a fall deeply monotonous. She had had enough of it. When she developed a chest infection she refused to go to hospital, wrapped herself tightly in a duvet and pretended to be asleep when a doctor came to give her antibiotics. I rang the next day; she assured me she was feeling much better, and died half an hour later.

But there was no chance of a completely simple, calm exit; that would have been entirely out of character. Some of the heroes in the novels and histories she loved die in hailstorms, or with attendant bolts of lightning. The sky darkens. Eagles fly over their deathbeds. In Larissa's case (she always loved a good mystery) someone broke into her empty house shortly after her death and set fire to it, causing a great deal of damage and nearly burning down the rest of the street. The police never found out who was responsible, or why they did it.

# Acknowledgements

Thanks for all sorts of help, advice and encouragement to:

Ruth Harris, Alex Pears, Michael Pears, Nick Penny, Lucy Katz, Michele Topham, Caroline Wood, Zoë Pagnamenta, Arabella Pike, Jill Bialosky, Kit Shepherd, Zara Moran, Nicholas Smith, Lyndal Roper, Keith Thomas, Elena Franklin, Colin Harrison, Eve Hutchings, Sam Harding, Lucy Tappin.

And, of course, Larissa.

# Dramatis Personae

Larissa Nikolaevna Salmina (1931–2024)
Francis James Herbert Haskell (1928–2000)

*Soviet Union*

Irina Antonova (1922–2020) director of the Pushkin Museum,
    Moscow, 1961–2013
Mikhail Artamonov (1898–1972) director of the State Hermitage
    Museum, Leningrad, 1951–64
Alexander Bakhchiev (1930–2007) pianist, and proposed
    husband of Larissa
Maya Bilikina, school friend of Larissa
Natasha Davidova, biologist, school friend of Larissa, witness at
    her wedding to Francis
Mikhail Dobroklonsky (1886–1964) academic supervisor of
    Larissa at the Hermitage Museum
Claudia Grechko (1907–1990) wife of Marshal Andrei Grechko
Tatyana Grechko (1927–2002) friend of Larissa in Ufa
Lev Gumilev (1912–1992) historian and anthropologist at the
    Hermitage Museum

Dolores Ibárruri (1895–1989) Spanish revolutionary known as
La Pasionaria, in exile in Ufa

Marta Kryzhanovskaya, friend of Larissa, curator of medieval
sculpture at the Hermitage Museum

Yury Kuznetsov, specialist in Dutch drawings at the Hermitage
Museum

Olga Lesnizkaya, fellow student of Larissa. Later curator of
Classical sculpture at the Hermitage Museum

Evgeny Lubo-Lesnichenko, specialist in Chinese textiles at the
Hermitage Museum. First love of Larissa

Viktor Mikhailov (1925–c.1968) naval officer, first husband of
Larissa

Jadviga Mikhailova, friend of Larissa's mother

Roma Muller, policeman, childhood friend of Larissa, witness at
her wedding to Francis

Ivan Salmin (d. 1928) army officer, Larissa's grandfather

Nikolai Salmin (1900–1961) army officer, Larissa's father

Yevgeny Salmin (1891–1969) naval officer, Larissa's uncle

Vera Salmina (1908–1987) Larissa's mother

Vsevolod Sofinsky, cultural attaché and KGB officer in London

Robert Spiegler (d. c.1954) engineer, lover of Larissa's mother

Igor Tarasov, art restorer at the Hermitage Museum, sent with
Larissa to the 1962 Venice Biennale

Leonid Tarassuk (1925–1990) keeper of arms and armour at the
Hermitage Museum

Vladislav Tregubov (c.1895–1952) Chief of Staff of air defences
during the siege of Leningrad

Mikhail Tukhachevskiy (1893–1937) military strategist, shot by
Stalin

Boris Veimarn (b. 1909) art critic

Irina Verblovskaya (1932–) Jewish school friend of Larissa,
imprisoned in 1957

Olga Zabotkina (1936–2001) ballet dancer and actress, school friend of Larissa

## England

Noel Annan, Baron Annan (1916–2000) military intelligence in the Second World War; Provost of King's College

Anthony Blunt (1907–1983) friend and colleague of Francis, Apostle, Soviet spy

Gerald Brooke (1938–) teacher arrested and tried for anti-Soviet activity while Francis and Larissa were trying to get married

Guy Burgess (1911–1963) Apostle, Soviet spy. Visited by Francis in 1963

Sir Harold Caccia (1905–1990) permanent under-secretary at the Foreign Office

George Cary (1928–1953) historian, school friend of Francis

Enid Margaret Cripps (1921–2006) author and philanthropist

Desmond Donnelly (1920–1974) Labour Member of Parliament

John Eyles (1923–2002) painter, friend of Francis

E. M. (Morgan) Forster (1879–1970) author, Apostle, fellow of King's College

Mark Frankland (1934–2012) journalist, Apostle, British spy

Ernst Gombrich (1909–2001) German-Jewish art historian; gave Francis's book a glowing review

Arnold Haskell (1903–1980) ballet critic, Francis's father

Emilie Mesritz Haskell (1881–1952) Francis's grandmother

Jacob Silas Haskell (1857–1938) banker, Francis's grandfather

Vera Zaitseva Haskell (1903–1968) Francis's mother

Dora Holzhandler (1928–2015) painter, girlfriend of Francis

Rosamond Lehmann (1901–1990) novelist and peripheral member of the Bloomsbury group

Benedict Nicolson (1914–1978) art historian, editor of the
*Burlington Magazine*, friend of Francis

Nikolaus Pevsner (1902–1983) German-Jewish art historian;
gave Francis the idea for his thesis

Paul Anthony Tanner (1935–1998) literary critic, fellow of
King's College after 1960 and friend of Francis

## *Europe*

Mark Aldanov (Landau) (1886–1957) émigré Russian novelist,
Francis's Uncle Max

Bernard Berenson (1865–1959) Latvian-Jewish-American art
historian, the most influential connoisseur of his age

Alessandro Bettagno (1919–2004) art historian, director of the
Fondazione Cini in Venice; matchmaker for Larissa and
Francis

Nina Bibikova (1929–2007) French-Ukrainian ballet dancer;
object of Francis's affections

Cécile Bondy (*c.*1890–1956) Francis's landlady in Paris

Rachel Bondy (b. 1912) her daughter

Countess Anna-Maria Cicogna Mozzoni (1913–2004) socialite

Marina Cicogna (1934–2023) her daughter; photographer,
socialite and film producer

Enzo Crea (*c.*1928–2007) photographer and publisher, friend of
Francis

Natalia Goncharova (1881–1962) émigré Russian Modernist
painter

Lyndall Passerini Hopkinson (b. 1931) friend of Francis in Rome

Renée-Marcelle (Zizi) Jeanmaire (1924–2020) French dancer
and TV personality; object of Francis's affections

Brigadier Brian Kennedy-Cooke (1894–1963) colonial
administrator, botanist, head of the British Council in Rome

Albert Clinton Landsberg (1889–1965) dilettante owner of the
Villa Malcontenta

Mikhail Larionov (1881–1964) Russian painter and set designer

Emanuele Macrì (1906–1973) Sicilian puppeteer

Alessandro Marabotti Marabottini (1926–2012) historian and
collector, friend of Francis

Umberto Morra di Lavriano (1897–1981) writer, journalist, anti-
fascist, friend of Francis

William Mostyn-Owen (1929–2011) art historian, fellow
Etonian, friend of Francis in Italy

Baron Nicolas de Plater (c.1880–1957) Russian émigré; Francis's
early guide to Paris

Luigi Salerno (1924–1992) art historian; shared flat with Francis
in Rome

Ugo Spirito (1896–1979) fascist sympathiser and philosopher

Meriel Stocker (c.1926–1976?) brief girlfriend of Francis in
Rome

# Notes

Most of the information presented here comes from two main sources: the audio recordings of Larissa's memoirs and Francis's diary. Larissa's account followed no particular order, and so a citation every time would serve no useful purpose. Francis's diary is referenced in the text. In addition, both wrote and received a huge number of letters. Those of Francis are with his other papers at the National Gallery in London, while Larissa's are deposited in the Taylorian Institute in Oxford. These are cited by date and author although, at the time of writing, neither collection has been sorted or catalogued. Finally, there are the voluminous notes which Francis wrote throughout his life – unpublished essays and book reviews, notes on buildings and paintings, character sketches of individuals and accounts of friends and colleagues. All of these were written more or less randomly, and again have not yet been catalogued. Quotations from these I cite as best I can.

## 1. Larissa: Background, Birth and Childhood, 1931–1941

1. See Sergei Grodzensky, *The Lubyanka Gambit* (London, Elk and Ruby Publishing, 2022), pp. 233–5.

## 2. Francis: Background, Birth and Education, 1928–1946

1. Eastern survived until it merged with Chartered Bank in 1957, which was then absorbed into Standard Chartered Plc in 1969. The bank's archives would have provided an exceptional record of the importance of finance in the Middle East and India in the late imperial period, had most of their contents not been destroyed in the 1980s. See S. G. H. Freeth, 'Destroying Archives: A Case Study of the Records of Standard Chartered Bank', *Journal of the Society of Archivists*, vol. 12, no. 2 (1991), pp. 85–94.
2. Arnold L. Haskell, *In His True Centre: An Interim Autobiography* (London, Adam & Charles Black, 1951), pp. 20–2.
3. *In His True Centre*, pp. 143–5; Arnold Haskell, *Balletomane at Large: An Autobiography* (London, Heinemann, 1972), p. 3.
4. Alicia Markova (1910–2004) was the first British ballerina to be internationally acclaimed. Arnold married her sister after his first wife died.
5. Haskell, *In His True Centre*, p. 65.
6. Anthony Sampson, *The Anatomy of Britain* (London, Hodder & Stoughton, 1962), p. 177.

## 3. Larissa: Siege, Evacuation, Return, 1941–1944

1. Hitler speech in Munich, 8 November 1941; directive 1601, issued 22 September 1941.
2. Marta also kept a diary of the siege, which is now at the E. P. Shaffe School in St Petersburg. I tried to get hold of a copy of this, but the invasion of Ukraine made that impossible. In it she recounts that 'so as not to cry, the children imagined themselves to be Indians "because Indians don't cry"'.
3. Tim Brinkhof, 'The Creatures That Devoured Leningrad', *History Today* online, 28 May 2020.
4. Maya's father was sent to Germany as the war ended to collect and bring back captured German scientists and engineers. The plane

crashed on landing, killing everyone on board. Larissa was convinced this was the work of the Americans.

5. Ibárruri also had to deal with the death of her son, reportedly killed at Stalingrad in September 1943, but who everyone in Ufa believed had been pushed out of a window in Moscow.

## 4. Francis: Paris, Army, Cambridge, 1946–1952

1. The new regime only lasted until 1958 – it kept out the Communists but was otherwise highly unstable, and it was then replaced (by de Gaulle) with a Fifth Republic that gave greatly enhanced powers to the presidency. Maurice Thorez (1900–1964) was the long-standing head of the French Communist Party.

2. Born Cécile Houdy, she was the first wife of the German artist and collector Walter Bondy, whom she had married after the birth of her daughter Rachel Andrée in 1912. She was connected to Otto Wacker, imprisoned in the 1930s for selling fake Van Goghs, and her company in Paris was called Wacker-Bondy. While she was hosting Francis she was being questioned about two paintings she had stored from the collection of the Dutch-Jewish collector Friedrich Gutmann. These had been confiscated by Bruno Lohse, responsible for looting works of art in Paris for Hitler. One, a School of Signorelli, was recovered in May 1946, but the other, a portrait by Dosso Dossi, was never seen again. The quotation comes from an essay Francis wrote describing his encounter with Rachel.

3. *New York Times*, 18 April 1943.

4. The Polonskis' son, Alexander – a close friend of Francis's – became a lawyer and accumulated a large archive documenting the cultural life of Russian exiledom.

5. Mikhail Larionov (1881–1964) left Russia with Diaghilev in 1915. Natalia Goncharova (1881–1962) moved to Paris in 1921. A leading figure of Russian Modernism. Francis's father had a large painting by her which Larissa gave to the Ashmolean Museum.

6. *Le Coq d'Or* (1908) ballet-opera by Rimsky-Korsakov. Produced in Paris by Fokine in 1914 with sets by Goncharova.

7. Boris Knyazev (1900–1975) born St Petersburg, left Russia in 1917 for Bulgaria, then moved to Paris in 1924 and opened a ballet school with his wife, Olga Spessivtseva. Alexander Tcherepnin (1899–1977)

born St Petersburg, left Russia for Georgia in 1917, moved to Paris in 1921, moved to the USA in 1948.

8. Presumably *Le Vendeur des Papillons*, unfinished ballet with music subsequently used by Tcherepnin as the third movement of his Third Symphony (1953).

9. The exchange rate in 1946 was about 500 francs to the pound, and 120 to the US dollar. For comparison, it had been 150 to the pound in 1939, and dropped still further to 1,300 in 1958. A reform in 1960 created the new franc, equal to 100 old francs, which lasted until the introduction of the euro. The weakness of the franc against the dollar in the interwar period had produced the phenomenon of the 'American in Paris' – fairly poor Americans living well in France – and also stoked the bitter suspicion of all things American which persists to this day.

10. *Les Enfants du Paradis*, directed by Marcel Carné (1943–5). *La Kermesse Héroïque*, directed by Jacques Feyder (1935); known as *Carnival in Flanders* in English. *L'Entraîneuse*, directed by Albert Valentin (1939), aka *The Nightclub Hostess* in English.

11. *Un Carnet de Bal* (*Life Dances On*) directed by Julien Duvivier (1937).

12. Charles Stewart Henry Vane-Tempest-Stewart, seventh Marquess of Londonderry (1878–1949). Nazi sympathiser and open anti-Semite, both of which spoiled an earlier reputation as a political moderate and supporter of the Royal Air Force. *Ourselves and Germany* was first published 1938. Goering and Ribbentrop were hanged at Nuremberg on 16 October 1946.

13. Joyce Cary (1888–1957) remains best known for *The Horse's Mouth*, the third of a trilogy of novels published between 1941 and 1944. Not to be confused with Joyce Carey, an actress Francis met at Cambridge in the 1950s, nor with George Carey the Archbishop of Canterbury. George Cary died at the age of 24 in 1953. His brother Tristram was a noted pioneer of electronic music, while his elder brother became a senior civil servant at the Ministry of Defence.

14. Miranda Carter, *Anthony Blunt: His Lives* (London, Macmillan, 2002), p. 104.

15. Notebook, 9 August 1980, commenting on David Newsome, *On the Edge of Paradise: A. C. Benson, the Diarist* (Chicago, University of Chicago Press, 1980).

16. Probably Anthony Lloyd, Baron Lloyd of Berwick, PC, DL, QC. Law lord between 1993 and his retirement in 1998.

17. Arthur Henry Hallam (1811–1833) was engaged to Tennyson's sister Emilia but had a closer friendship with Tennyson himself, who considered him 'as near perfection as mortal man could be'. Tennyson dedicated his greatest poem, *In Memoriam* (1850), to him. The lines ''Tis better to have loved and lost,/Than never to have loved at all' encapsulate the emotions involved.

18. Margaret Ann Phipps (1925–2009). Margaret's father was Sir Eric Phipps (1875–1945), who was Ambassador to both Germany and France in the 1930s. He retired to his Wiltshire estate in 1939 and died two days after VJ Day.

19. Renée-Marcelle Jeanmaire (1924–2020) now remembered in the Anglo-Saxon world mainly for a line in a 1960s song: 'You talk like Marlene Dietrich/and you dance like Zizi Jeanmaire …'

20. Enid Margaret Cripps (1921–2006) children's author and philanthropist, daughter of Labour Chancellor of the Exchequer Sir Stafford Cripps. Her marriage in June 1953 – shortly after the coronation – to the Ghanaian lawyer and politician Joe Appiah was the social sensation of the year. To give him his due, Francis swiftly came to appreciate and like her enormously; 'She has a charming laugh, and her personality is irresistibly pleasant.'

21. Such as Arnold Wesker's play *Chips with Everything* (1962) on the serious social commentary side; on the more frivolous side *The Army Game* (1957–61), the first sitcom produced on the new independent channel ITV.

22. Of the Bloomsbury group, E. M. Forster was the only surviving member at King's. The economist John Maynard Keynes (who transformed the college's finances) died in 1946.


## 5. Larissa: School, Academy, Hermitage, 1944–1962

1. O. A. Platonov (ed.), *The Black Hundred, An Historical Encyclopaedia, 1900–1917* (Moscow, A. D. Stepanov, 2008).

2. Geraldine Norman, *The Hermitage: The Biography of a Great Museum* (London, Jonathan Cape, 1997), pp. 330–49. By far the best book written in English on the history of the Hermitage and on the museum's importance.

3. Mikhail Artamonov (1898–1972) director of the Hermitage 1951–64; Boris Piotrovsky (1908–1990) director 1964–90; Mikhail Piotrovsky (1974–) director 1990 to the present.

## 6. Francis: Italy, 1952–1962

1. A few of his parents' acquaintances did pass through, and Francis was given the task of taking them around Rome: 'to Hotel Continentale to meet Irene Skorik. Mario insisted on coming. Like all Italians he thinks that Ballerina and Prostitute are virtually synonyms' (8 February 1952).
2. Quoted by Louise Rice in Richard Shone and John-Paul Stonard (eds), *The Books That Shaped Art History: From Gombrich and Greenberg to Alpers and Krauss* (London, Thames & Hudson, 2013), p. 149.
3. The botanical papers of Kennedy-Cooke (1894–1963) are now at Durham University. Until 2006, the British Council in Rome was based in the very handsome Palazzo Albani del Drago in the via Quattro Fontane. It then moved to a dreary modern building in the suburbs, where it now tries to shake off the image which had worked so well for so long.
4. Lyndall Hopkinson's own account of this period is in her book *Nothing to Forgive: A Daughter's Life of Antonia White* (London, Chatto & Windus, 1988), pp. 339–67.
5. I encountered Maria Francesca Tiepolo (1925–2020) myself when doing research in Venice many years ago. I described what I wanted. She looked at me with a withering pity, ignored everything I said, and then ordered me up the volumes of material I should have been asking for. Immensely helpful, deeply charming, utterly terrifying.
6. This was Jill Pratt (1921–2009), whose remarkable life is documented by her son, François Grosjean, in *A la recherche de Roger et Sallie* (Hauterive, Switzerland, Editions Attinger, 2016).
7. Luigi Salerno (1924–1992) art historian and civil servant; specialist on Salvator Rosa, Guercino and other Baroque painters. Also lived in Sandro Marabottini's flat with Francis.
8. Ugo Spirito (1896–1979) fascist sympathiser and philosopher whose left-wing economic views ultimately led to a falling out with Mussolini.
9. Emanuele Macrì (1906–1973) succeeded his master and adoptive father Don Mariano Pennisi in 1934. The boy was probably his son Salvatore, who fell in love with an American heiress and introduced Sicilian puppetry to the United States in the 1960s. Emanuele's theatre in Acireale, the Teatro Pennisi di Pupi Siciliani, is the only surviving example of traditional Sicilian puppet theatre.

10. Quoted in Caterina Zappia (ed.), *Collezione Alessandro Marabottini* (Rome, De Luca editori d'arte, 2016), p. 17.

## 7. Larissa and the Biennale, 1962

1. Interview with Geraldine Norman in Nikolai Molok (ed.), *Russian Artists at the Venice Biennale* (Moscow, Stella Art Foundation, 2013), pp. 297–381.
2. Matteo Bertelé, 'Soviet "Severe Romanticism" at the 1962 Venice Biennale: The Case of Viktor Popkov', *Experiment*, vol. 23 (2017), pp. 158–72.
3. See Peter Kozorezenko, *Viktor Popkov, Russian Painter of Genius* (London, Unicorn, 2013). Since the fall of the Soviet Union, Popkov's reputation has dramatically improved, and his paintings are greatly sought after.
4. Eleonory Gilburd, *To See Paris and Die: The Soviet Lives of Western Culture* (Cambridge, MA, Belknap Press, 2018), pp. 158–60.
5. Alessandro Bettagno (1919–2004) specialist on Italian eighteenth-century art, especially Venetian. Secretary then director of the Fondazione Cini in Venice.
6. Beverley Nichols, quoted in Andrew Mead, 'La Malcontenta 1924–1939: Tumult and Order', *Architects' Journal*, 26 November 2012.

## 8. Francis: London and Cambridge, 1953–1962

1. Francis wrote up the entire period in one go when he left the job in mid-1954, and all quotations come from this single, unpaginated, essay.
2. That was perceptive of Donnelly. The law decriminalising homosexuality in England was eventually passed in 1967, when Labour had a majority of ninety-eight.
3. The debate was on 28 April 1954. The first public protest against the laws had been in 1950. The main speech demanding decriminalisation was given by the Conservative MP Robert Boothby. In August, the government set up a Royal Commission to investigate and the Wolfenden report recommending decriminalisation was published in 1957.
4. Ian Grimble (1921–1994) broadcaster, author and lifelong advocate of all things Scottish. Roger Morgan (1926–2018) son of the author and

playwright Charles Langbridge Morgan. Like Francis also from Eton, he joined the library as a temporary measure, but never left and later became chief librarian.

5. Paul Anthony Tanner (1935–1998) specialist in American literature; fellow of King's for much of his career.

6. Perhaps because this age was coming to an end, the period saw a rich crop of fictional memorials to the English upper middle classes, particularly the ten-volume *Alms for Oblivion* series (1964–76) by Francis's friend Simon Raven (King's Cambridge) and Anthony Powell's (Eton) twelve-volume *Dance to the Music of Time* (1951–75).

7. Rosamond Lehmann (1901–1990) novelist and peripheral member of the Bloomsbury group, married Walter Runciman, then Wogan Phillips. Hugo, her son by Phillips, became a friend of Francis (and the only member of the Communist Party to sit in the House of Lords). Garry Runciman, Walter's son by his second marriage, became another close friend. Bernard Berenson (1865–1959) a Latvian-Jewish-American art historian, was the most influential connoisseur of his age and since the 1920s had been holding court at I Tatti, his villa outside Florence. The introduction was a great prize, although Francis found him disappointingly petulant.

8. Countess Anna-Maria Cicogna Mozzoni (Venice 1913–2004) daughter of the fabulously wealthy Giuseppe Volpe di Misurata (1877–1947) who founded the Venice Film Festival.

9. Marina Cicogna (1934–2023) photographer, socialite and producer of the classic movie *Belle de Jour*.

## 9. Meeting, 1962

1. For comparison, the average working wage in 1962 was £832 per year; an MP was paid £1,000, a teacher £1,244 and an NHS doctor £2,387.

2. And so there was. My heart went out to him for that one.

3. E. H. Gombrich, 'A Golden Age of Patronage', *Observer*, 23 June 1963. Reprinted as 'Patrons and Painters in Baroque Italy', in E. H. Gombrich, *Reflections on the History of Art: Views and Reviews*, ed. Richard Woodfield (Oxford, Phaidon, 1987), pp. 106–8.

4. Rudolf Nureyev (1938–1993) Russian ballet dancer who spectacularly defected to the West in June 1961.

5. Trattoria in Castello, not far from the Biennale. Larissa's favourite. Good fish.

6. Nino Dramis (1928–1997) Calabrian writer of short stories, some of which were published by Enzo Crea's publishing firm, Le Edizioni dell'Elefante.
7. *L'ideale classico del Seicento in Italia e la pittura di paesaggio*, Palazzo dell'Archiginnasio, Bologna, 8 September–11 November 1962.
8. 'The nicest hotel I have ever been to. Utterly unpretentious from the outside, wonderfully comfortable, marvellous food and totally, totally, peaceful. Never have I felt so happy and relaxed.' The Cipriani still gets really good ratings.
9. They remained friends, however; Meriel got a job working for the *Oxford Times* in the late 1950s and commissioned a few articles from Francis.
10. Benedict Nicolson (1914–1978) art historian and editor of the *Burlington Magazine*. Not to be confused with Ben Nicholson the painter (1894–1982).

## 10. Encounters, 1963–1965

1. George (Dadie) Rylands (1902–1999) literary scholar and theatre director.
2. Boris Vladimirovich Veimarn, born 1909 in Sevastopol. Art historian and critic. Author of *The Ideological Unity and National Diversity of Soviet Art* (1962) and works on Central Asian art.
3. See 'Dall'URSS a Ca' Pesaro un quadro di Matisse', *Il Gazzettino*, 26 June 1962; 'Una Stima inesatta consente il ritorno di un quadro a Mosca', *Ivi*, 23 October 1962.
4. The friendship of Britten, Dimitri Shostakovich and the cellist Mstislav Rostropovich was a major cultural link during the Cold War until Britten's death in 1976. See Alexander Rossinsky and Ekaterina Vorontsova, 'Benjamin Britten in the Music Culture of the Soviet Union in the 1960s', *International Journal of Humanities and Social Science*, vol. 3, no. 14 (2013), pp. 166–9.
5. Philby's defection also blew the cover of David Cornwell as a member of MI6, then serving in Germany. He resigned and took up full-time writing under his pseudonym of John le Carré.
6. Wilfrid Scawen Blunt, *My Diaries: Being a Personal Narrative of Events, 1888–1914* (New York, Knopf, 1923), vol. 1, p. 53.
7. Noel Annan, Baron Annan (1916–2000) military intelligence in the Second World War; Provost of King's College Cambridge and then

of University College London; Vice-Chancellor of the University of London; author of the Annan report on the future of broadcasting; etc., etc.

8. Michael Barber, *Captain: The Life and Times of Simon Raven* (London, Duckworth, 1996), p. 84.

9. Julian Bell, born 1908, son of Clive and Vanessa Bell, nephew of Virginia Woolf. Lover of Anthony Blunt, member of the Apostles. Went against his parents' advice to Spain during the civil war to work as an ambulance driver and was killed by a bomb in July 1937. Burgess's role in sending Bell to Spain is unclear.

10. Italian restaurant in Charlotte Street, Soho. Introduced Italian cuisine to London before the Second World War.

11. Sir Philip Dennis Proctor (1905–1983) Treasury civil servant.

12. Lev Gumilev (1912–1992) historian and anthropologist, son of the poet Anna Akhmatova. His father Nikolai, also a poet, was executed in 1921, and he was held in prison from 1938 to 1943 and from 1949 to 1953 for no particular reason. He was hired by Artamonov as a librarian on his release after Stalin's death.


## 11. Departure and Arrival, 1965

1. The dilemma was not a new one – in July 1838, as he contemplated proposing to his cousin Emma Wedgwood, Charles Darwin listed the alternatives. Under 'Marry' he included: '... Constant companion, (& friend in old age) who will feel interested in one ... better than a dog anyhow ... Charms of music & female chit-chat. – These things good for one's health. – *but terrible loss of time.*' 'Not Marry' included: 'Freedom to go where one liked ... Conversation of clever men at clubs – Not forced to visit relatives, & to bend in every trifle ...'

2. Sofinsky went on to be spokesman for the Foreign Ministry, then Soviet Ambassador to New Zealand (from which he was expelled in 1980), and finished his career at the United Nations as part of the Soviet delegation. It was the New Zealand intelligence service which concluded that, far from being a career diplomat, he was in reality a long-term member of the KGB. He later gained a reputation for his hardline approach to relations with the West. See Murray Seeger, 'Eye-Witness to History', in Leonard Schapiro and Joseph Godson (eds), *The Soviet Worker: Illusions and Realities* (London, Macmillan, 1981), p. 80.

3. Bibikova was finally allowed out of the Soviet Union to join Matthews in England in January 1966, a month after Larissa left Russia. The couple's story was recounted in a wonderful book by their son, Owen Matthews: *Stalin's Children, Three Generations of Love and War* (London, Bloomsbury, 2008).

4. This and all the following quotations are from an extended, 46-page entry Francis wrote in his diary in Helsinki between 15 and 17 August 1965.

# Index

Illustrations are denoted by the use of *italic* page numbers. Francis Haskell and Larissa Salmina Haskell are denoted by FH and LH respectively.

# Index

Bartolomeo Pinelli, *Il Riposo dell'Autore: Tutto finisce*, 1809